THE OLIVE PICKER
A Memoir

Kathryn Brettell

Jazz Dog Press

Conifer, Colorado

Kathryn Brettell/Jazz Dog Press
Conifer, Colorado 80433
www.theolivepicker.com

Book Layout © 2014 BookDesignTemplates.com

The Olive Picker/ Kathryn Brettell. -- 1st ed.
ISBN 978-0-9861929-0-6

To Peter, without you this book might never have been written.

Disclaimer

To write this book, I relied upon my personal journals, researched facts when I could, consulted with several of the people who appear in the book, called upon my own recollection of these events and these times of my life and have related them to the best of my memory and knowledge. I have changed the names of some but not all of the individuals in this book. There are no composite characters or events in this book. I occasionally omitted people and events, but only when that omission had no impact on either the veracity or the substance of the story.

CONTENTS

CHAPTER ONE

October 8, 2008

Perfect billowy white clouds look pasted against the clear azure sky. A cool breeze tickles my cheek. Six strong arms hold me steady as they push the gurney across the street in front of my home. My beautiful view is then rudely interrupted as I am loaded like cargo into the waiting ambulance. Now, with only a metal ceiling to look at, I strain to hear the paramedic call out my blood pressure. I watch him adjust the IV's roller clamp, previously just a drip, to increase the flow into my arm and I feel the warmed fluid spread throughout my thirsty veins. Closing my eyes, I try to concentrate on his words, hopeful they'll distract me from the pictures that hold a pitbull-like grip on my mind.

"Multiple head wounds, BP...O2 sat..."

I can't stay focused.

How could such a horrible thing happen on this beautiful day?

I hear the driver ask from the front seat, "do you think she'll make it?"

"Doesn't look good," answers the man leaning over me.

I'm right here, I can hear you.

"Try to get some contact info," the driver responds nonchalantly, and the ambulance begins to move, the wailing siren signaling someone aboard.

Funny how the sirens aren't as loud from inside the bus.

In my mind, I see smeared blood on the walls, and some pooled on the floor in the bathroom. I try to shut that out, try to think of something else. My legs start to shake uncontrollably again, soon my whole body joins in.

Neurogenic tremors. I'd witnessed the phenomenon many times when I worked the Emergency Room. Innate to all mammals after a trauma, it's the natural response of a shocked or disrupted nervous system attempting to thaw out or release itself from the freeze response and become fully functional again.

Will I ever be fully functional again?

"Is there anyone we can call?" The medic holds the oxygen mask off my face, and waits for my answer.

Really? Are you serious?

Until this moment, I never appreciated how difficult it is for trauma patients to answer questions. My jaw is shoved to the right at an unnatural angle. If somehow I survive I vow to be more considerate when I need patient information and remember to ask only those questions with yes or no answers.

"My dauler," is the best I can say.

He replaces the mask.

"Do you have her number?"

Well, there's a yes or no question.

I wonder if anyone has thought to grab my purse, find my phone, and look at my contacts. What would they do if I was already dead?

Bending my hands at the wrists I struggle to hold up shaking, bloody fingers as I speak, my arms strapped down at my sides. I hope the numbers stay in my head long enough to pass along the information.

"Eyn, do, sree." The effort is exhausting, and my brain is only able to visualize the numbers in sets. Once the next set materializes I continue, "Four, sick, sick, vive." It would have been helpful if he'd taken the oxygen mask off again.

We move along roads that, until today, have been totally familiar to me. Now, facing backward and lying down I'm not sure where I am.

I shut my eyes and the scenes begin again, returning home from work...a glass of wine. I let the tape roll...watching *Dancing with the Stars*...the Presidential debate...

"923-4665?" He repeats.

Amazing. This guy is good.

"Yeth."

The ambulance rocks and catches every bump; corners are the worst.

Waking up too early...falling back to sleep. Sitting on the bed...in the dark...

"No answer, do you have anyone else?"

"No."

Why did I say no? I have friends.

The darkness of the bedroom...falling back to sleep...

Focus, I tell myself. I'm in Texas. My older sister Debbie lives in Louisiana. My daughter lives just a couple of miles from me, and my son, in New Mexico. Everyone else is in California. Rod's family lives in Iowa. My best friends, Curt and LeAndra are in Howe, a Texas town forty miles away. I can't think of anyone's phone number; a sad consequence of cell phones and speed dial. Bruce, maybe. My daughter's husband.

"No one?" He repeats, and mercifully raises the mask again.

"Shun-in-law Bruush Landwy. Erks at Hess South. Don't know a nummer." Speaking requires so much effort, and I'm tired. I feel myself drifting.

That's good, my brain needs a rest; my eyelids are like lead. I yield to the gentle bumps rocking me. I hear foggy voices, and a little girl giggling far, far away.

Wind rushes past my face in a steady rhythm, first blowing my hair back away from my face, then forward covering my eyes. I can barely breathe in one direction, and can't stop laughing in the other. Through squinting eyes I see sunlight dance off distant water. Brilliant colors of green and blue blur as the landscape blends together in equal parts. As gravity pulls me backward in free-fall, I draw in a breath and am aware of the rich aroma of sun baked hay. I continue moving in that gentle arc, stopping briefly suspended in space, before being pushed forward again. The swing begins its ascent and I hear myself laugh as the wind rushes past my face in its warm and perfect caress. My dad, behind me, pushes me higher and higher. It is a beautiful day.

\#

My Dad liked to play basketball. He wasn't famous or even extra good at it, but he played well enough that he got a job coaching high-school basketball in northern California. One weekend he picked up Debbie and me and took us to the Sacramento State College gym where the Harlem Globetrotters were running practice drills. He knew all the Globetrotters, and in particular, was friends with Meadowlark

Lemon. Meadowlark was the biggest man I'd ever seen. I remember watching his head come down from the sky as he bent and asked if I played basketball too. I shook my head no. Then he asked if I knew how to dunk, and I again shook my head no.

"Oh, I *know* you can dunk!" Meadowlark boomed, and scooped me up in one quick sweep of his enormous hand, planting me on his shoulders, my scrawny legs dangling in front of his chest like a pair of braids.

It was fascinating to be up that high—like being on top of the world. Meadowlark told me to hang on and I wrapped my arms tight around his sweaty forehead as he carefully moved across the court. He was incredibly strong, with powerful shoulders, and I could feel his neck muscles ripple as he moved. It was amazing.

When he got close to the basket he handed the ball up to me. "Dunk it," he commanded. I hardly had to stretch–the ball dropped easily through the net. The whole gym erupted in a cheer and I remember smiling so big my face hurt. It was one of the happiest days of my life.

Usually our Dad's weekends involved Debbie and me watching him play tennis or basketball while we played under a tree, or dug holes in the ground with sticks, or read the comic books we had just gotten from Wombles Drug Store, or any combination of otherwise "good girl" activities that involved keeping quiet and watching him have fun. So, being the center of attention was a unique event. My mother always said, "Good little girls are seen and not heard," a common mantra in the 1950s culture, and one I endeavored to fulfill. I tried to be a good, quiet little girl, even invisible when I could be, unlike Debbie who was loud even when she tried to be quiet.

Looking back, I recognize that my mother was chock full of bad advice

.

CHAPTER TWO

The Therapist
September 2000

Along the interior wall, the one opposite the window, sat a well-worn couch. Not too low to the ground, but not too high for short people to sit and still have their feet touch the floor. It was upholstered in beige corduroy, a material meant not to offend anyone. The entire office was subtly calming, from the shaded window blocking direct light, to the soft neutral colors, to the large Om yoga symbol staring at me from the bookcase. I silently mouthed the Om chant. It didn't help calm me.

The things that were absent were more noticeable. There were no personal pictures in the bookcase. No candles. No telephone on the desk that would distract her. I looked at the space on the floor and wondered if she did yoga poses when she didn't have clients; she looked the type. There was a distinct lack of odor.

Well, what did I expect; home-baked cookies?

I sat at the end of the couch nearest her desk. Conscious she would be monitoring my actions, I wanted to project confidence. Aware I had crossed my legs, I quickly uncrossed them. She came into the room and sat, positioning her chair at the side of her desk. We made eye contact. "So, how does this work?" I asked, wanting to get on with it. No sense fiddling around.

"Well, why don't you start by telling me why you're here?" She leaned back in her chair and folded her hands in her lap.

Well, at least one of us is comfortable.

Her question annoyed me. Certainly she had a report of some sort, it hadn't been my idea to be there.

"Um, well, I guess Dr. Saad, or whoever...was afraid I would...kill myself," a wave rushed through me as I spoke the words. I smiled, then worried it might look fake, so I chuckled to cover my discomfort.

"Will you?"

Would I?

I hadn't actually thought about it. I guess after what had happened, somebody seemed to think I might. *Why did they think that? Had I done something I didn't remember?* I realized the delay in my answer would be noticed.

"No.

The word sounded so inadequate, so quiet. *The word 'no' has such a big meaning, why is it such a little word?* I cleared my throat and tried again. "No," and combined it with a small shake of my head. I felt stiff and tense. I could hear the clock on her desk ticking. *Are these walls soundproof?*

"Why don't you tell me about yourself?" she asked, "then maybe we can figure out why you're here."

That didn't sound threatening. It was an opening, of sorts. I looked over at her shaded window across from my seat on the

THE OLIVE PICKER · 9

couch. I'd never really thought about why anything had happened. I was 47 years old, and I had just let life drag me along in its wake. Now I realized I desperately wanted to know why this thing had happened. It had been so unusual for me, so unexpected.

"Well, like, where do I start, what do you want to know?" I laughed nervously.

"Everything. I want to hear everything. The beginning is usually the best place to start," she smiled. "It's all connected, so let's start at the beginning."

We spent every Wednesday from 2:00 to 3:00 o'clock, for the next twelve months, talking about me. Just me.

Everything I was about to tell her was the truth, to the best of my memory. But even though patterns appeared and reappeared, neither she nor I could have predicted what would happen after we ended our sessions.

CALIFORNIA

CHAPTER THREE

Step-Monster

My mom wasn't comfortable around little kids, and she expected a lot from us. A taskmaster, she insisted we make our beds with mitered corners even before we were old enough to go to school. Debbie and I delivered on her expectations, we did what she asked and didn't cause trouble, and Mom often commented that we could be counted on to do the right thing. Our mom must have worked different shifts because some mornings she slept while Debbie and I made our own breakfasts and lunches and got ourselves off to school, and other mornings she had already gone to work when we woke up.

Debbie and I shared a bedroom until we left home. She was 16 months older than me, and had been born on the fourth of July. Debbie was loud and boisterous as a firecracker compared to me. I often wished I was as brave or smart and could speak out and ask questions the way she did.

We were poor. Not horrendously poor, but certainly lacking. After our parents divorced, we lived with our mom in a succession of rat-infested houses. Mom finally rented out my bed to a college student for extra money, which meant I had to sleep on the couch. I didn't know we were poor at the time, I thought every kid ate shit on a shingle or potato chip casserole for dinner, had to walk around the mice scattering across the floor to get to their high chairs, then slept on the couch. We weren't homeless and I'm certain it was the best she could do at the time. She worked full time and as a divorced, single mother of two small children in the mid-1950s, it couldn't have been easy.

Mom's parents finally stepped in and co-signed on a cute little house on 52nd street in Sacramento for the three of us. It was a square two-bedroom house with a single bathroom and had a big backyard, all on a nice, quiet street, with no mice. It had a detached garage and a kitchen with an old-time gas range. It was cute and just right for Mom, Debbie, and me.

Mom saw other men after the divorce, but she complained she could never get past a first date. She blamed Debbie and me for that. She said we scared them off. She said no decent man wanted damaged goods with baggage.

In the summer of 1958, she got involved with the man who would become our stepfather. I was five years old and about to start into the first grade. Debbie and I had ridden our bikes to El Dorado Elementary School every day the previous year and always minded the traffic lights. We knew well enough how to get ourselves to school by then.

Bob was about as tall as our real father had been, except he had blonde hair that he wore in an Elvis pompadour. He usually wore jeans and a white t-shirt. He was moody; he didn't like being asked questions, and he rarely gave answers. He didn't like kids. Mom told us not to bother him.

When Bob was around we had to either go play in our room or go outside and stay out until the streetlights came on, which was the normal summer rule for all the kids on our block. We played all sorts of games or rode our bikes or read from our collection of comic books. There were loads of kids in that neighborhood and on the adjoining streets who rode bikes, and we had plenty of things to do to keep us away from the house.

School was back in session that fall, and Debbie and I got back into our routine fast. Debbie made our standard breakfasts of one hardboiled egg each, and my job was to pack our lunches which were the very same every day. I made a peanut butter and jelly sandwich, put half in each bag, with two cookies each. We double checked to be sure we had made our beds, then we got our bikes out of the garage and walked to the street in front of the house.

This particular morning, we started to cross the street like we had done a million times before, when suddenly we heard Bob's voice from inside the house telling us to come back. By his tone it sounded important. Up until he yelled, I hadn't even realized he was at our house, but then again I wasn't surprised. I looked and saw his car in the driveway. Mom's car was gone.

We threw our bikes on the lawn, and went in through the front door to look for him. We found him standing in the kitchen staring out the window that overlooked the back yard and garage. He took Debbie's arm and said he wanted to show her something. I started to follow, but he told me to wait in the kitchen. I was disappointed, but did as I was told and watched them walk out across the back yard.

They walked like that, him holding her arm. They got to the garage and almost as soon as they'd gone inside and closed the door, I heard Debbie scream. The sound ripped through me like a knife. I started toward the back door, to go see what was wrong, but stopped because I was scared. I remembered I'd been told to wait.

The screams were piercing, and I began to feel weak, my heart thumped hard against my chest. Finally, the garage door opened and they came out. He still held her upper arm but now Debbie wasn't walking very well, and I could see she was upset. Her face was blotchy and wet. He dragged her across the patio and in through the back door to the kitchen. Panicked, I asked what had happened, but Debbie was crying with snot bubbling on her face and Bob roughly pushed me away. I followed them down the hall, and timidly asked again what had happened. He dragged Debbie to the bedroom that she and I shared, pushed her in, and shut the door. Then he turned back to me.

"C'mon," he said and reached for my arm.

"What's out there?" I was only five years old and the most horrible thing I could think of was there must be a big ugly spider in the garage and the thought made my stomach tight and fear thickened my throat. I fought back tears.

That was the first time I noticed the difference in his eyes– those ice blue eyes that Mom said were so pretty had changed. Now they looked flat and empty.

"C'mon," he repeated quietly and took my arm.

"No. No, NO, NO," I pulled back and tried to get away, and when I couldn't, I fought. I was in full panic, uselessly jumping and pulling against him all the way out to the garage, screaming, "I don't want to see the spider."

As soon as we were inside the garage I saw Bob reach up on a shelf. I was sure that was where the spider was and new fear swept over me. I screamed louder and fought even harder, hitting him with my free hand, and trying to peel his fingers off my arm. But his grip on my skinny limb was solid. When I felt the first stings on my legs my brain exploded with the thought that there wasn't one, but hundreds of spiders. He held my arm even harder as he chased me round in circles, my legs and buttocks being thrashed over and over with what I could finally see was a two-foot-long horsewhip.

My cotton dress offered no protection. I don't know how long the whipping lasted, but I woke up hours later on my mom's bed, my legs bloody and badly bruised. My arm felt like it was no longer part of my body. I wondered if Debbie was still alive.

I fell back to sleep and when I woke again I could tell it was late in the day as the room had taken on a shadow, but I still didn't get off the bed. I could hear Mom and Bob talking in low voices. I wondered what he told her had happened. A short time later Mom opened her bedroom door and said I was allowed out to eat dinner.

I felt achy and sore as I got off the bed and shuffled my way to the kitchen. I was relieved to see Debbie already at the table. The back of my thighs stung when I sat down, and they stuck to the plastic chair. I sat facing the garage. I had no appetite. I felt sick. Mom never asked Debbie or me anything about what happened, but as she sat down at the head of the table opposite Bob she said, "Next time I bet you'll look both ways before crossing the street."

Bob was a monster, but I had always looked to my mother for protection, and her betrayal was a far worse realization. In the flash of an instant, it seemed, she decided he was more important to her than Debbie and me.

CHAPTER FOUR

Set Adrift

Bob was mean to our mom, too. I hadn't seen him hit her, but I didn't like the way he said things that hurt her feelings. Sometimes she tried to laugh so we wouldn't know he was being mean, but we knew. We weren't stupid.

They got married in our grandparent's garden, July 5, 1959, when I was six years old, having dated for less than a year. Mom wore a pink-fitted dress and they looked at each other with happy smiles during the ceremony.

Afterwards, Bob took Debbie and me aside and said that he was our father now, and we needed to change our last name to his. Debbie asked if he had adopted us, and he admitted that he hadn't. She asked him if our real father knew about us changing our names, and Bob said that didn't matter. Debbie frowned. Bob quickly promised that on my thirteenth birthday, he would formally adopt both of us and make the name change legal. But in the meantime, our new last name was Ross; I was Kathi Ross now, and he said I had to start using that name at school immediately.

Then he made another rule: he said because he wasn't our *real* father, he would only take care of us until we were eighteen years old or graduated high school–whichever came first–then we had to leave home. Eighteen years old seemed like a long time away, and I wasn't as worried about that rule as I was about changing my name. With the name change, that branch of our family tree was severed forever. No more birthday cards, no Christmas presents. No further contact with our father or his parents, no more summer visits to their house on the beach. We were set adrift with new identities, the only sign of our previous lives were the steady checks in the mail for child support sent monthly by our real father for our care – until we were eighteen years old or graduated high school.

In September, Mom and Bob took a belated weekend honeymoon in Las Vegas while Mom's mother looked after us. When they got home Bob said they had a couple of surprises. We each got a beaded leather belt that said Lake Tahoe across the back, but we were going to have to guess what the second surprise was.

We went through a million clues, and finally narrowed it down to it being smaller than a bread box, something alive that would grow bigger, and it could live inside the house but could go outside too. It had to be a dog I thought, or even better, a puppy. A German Shepherd maybe. I had always wanted a dog and with all these perfect clues, there was nothing else it could be except a puppy.

It was a baby all right, just not a baby dog. I was absolutely heartbroken. A new brother or sister was little consolation.

I loved horses even more than I loved dogs and nearly every game Debbie and I made up involved horses. We played Wagon Train on our twin beds with two suitcases. One case was made of brown leather that I named Buck. The other was a snakeskin case with my Mom's initials stamped under the handle. That one I named Snake. I tied jump ropes to the handles on the cases and with them, I drove the "horses" while I sat on the end of the bed. I was always the wagon driver and Debbie was the mom in the back of the wagon taking care of the babies. We could play for hours and hours by ourselves.

I had a small collection of five or six plastic horse statues that sat on the window next to my bed, and everyone knew that if I had one wish to make on a wishbone, one penny to throw in the pond, or one prayer to send to God, I would be wishing for a horse.

In November, on my seventh birthday, Bob took me to Selby's Stables in Sacramento. I was told we were going to look at some horses. I raced to put on my jeans, checkered western shirt with the fancy snaps, and my beaded Lake Tahoe belt. Mom braided my hair. I looked at myself in the mirror and was satisfied with my reflection. I looked just like Annie Oakley.

When we got to the stable, I could see the horses' legs on the other side of a nearby fence. Climbing the boards, I discovered it held a whole pen full of horses. They were gorgeous. They had wooly hair, their tails flicked back and forth swatting flies, occasionally one blew snot, and they just walked around being horses. The sun shone in rays and I could see the dust and horse hair floating in the air. I could have stayed for days watching them move around the pen. The thick horse smell was intoxicating. I loved them all and was picturing any one of them standing in our back yard and speculated how big a bucket I would need to buy for feed and water.

Bob's voice fractured my daydream as he called me over where he was. I didn't want to leave just yet and I lingered until he called again.

Bob was standing beside a man who held the reins of a big gray horse, and the man asked if I was ready to get on. I hesitated, then nodded furiously. I wasn't expecting to actually get to sit on a horse. I'd never been on one before and Bob had only said we would look at them. The man picked me up and put me on the saddle. When I started shaking, I worried I might fall off. The man put his hand on my leg, and asked if I was okay. I nodded tentatively, and realized I felt much better with him holding onto me, and I hoped he would stay there for a little while, but he walked away. I started shaking again, and tried to calm my nerves by telling myself that Annie Oakley didn't shake like a bowl of jelly when she was on a horse. I told myself to be brave but I was really nervous. Luckily the big gray didn't move a hair. His feet seemed rooted to the spot, and I soon wondered if he could move at all.

Meanwhile, Bob was being outfitted with another beautiful horse. His was dark brownish red with a black mane and tail, and everything seemed to be going well until Bob noticed the horse only had one eye. According to Bob this was a huge insult, and he demanded a different horse immediately. He yelled that he wasn't paying to ride a fleabag horse that only had one eye, and by God, they had a whole pen full, so they just needed to get him another one and be quick about it. I wished he would shut up. He was making the horse feel bad. If I could just talk to that horse, I'd tell him Bob was an ass and sometimes mean, but sometimes he was nice too. Like today, who would have thought he would bring me to ride a horse for the very first time in my life?

Bob should have kept the one-eyed horse. The one he chose to ride—after walking around it like he was buying a car—moved at the speed of a snail. Even the big gray I was riding walked faster, especially when we turned around and he could see the barn. Then he ran like Man-O-War's cousin. It was a day I would never forget and I vowed to rethink my attitude toward Bob.

#

Debbie looked forward to the new baby with an excitement I just didn't share. When Debbie asked Mom where the baby would sleep (I hadn't cared), she was delighted to learn they were planning on putting the crib in our room. It was already a small room, with just our two twin beds and a tiny bookcase for our comic books. Mom and Bob assembled the secondhand crib in the living room, and I was thrilled when they discovered it wouldn't go through the bedroom door. Angry and yelling, Bob took it apart again and reassembled it inside our room in the space between our beds. When it was all put together, it stood at the foot of our beds, in the exact space where Buck and Snake needed to be in order to pull our wagon train. I stared at that spot for a long time. I wasn't pleased at all.

It was born in June, and, oh my God, did Bob love that baby. When they brought it home from the hospital, even though the car was hotter than the inside of an oven, Mom and the little darling weren't allowed to get out until Bob got his camera ready and took at least a dozen pictures. Then he snatched the baby away from her. He chattered away in baby talk and made up words, and when he held it he curved his back and shoulders forward and walked real slow. It was a girl, and he said they had named her Janie Kay, after some long lost mysterious aunt of his who supposedly lived in England. The way he talked about the old aunt I thought she must have been royalty.

We were told we had to wash our hands with a special soap before we could meet Janie, and Debbie ran right into the bathroom and got busy. I refused. I really didn't care to see the baby. Mom told Bob, "She's got her nose out of joint," a comment I thought was stupid. My nose was just fine and if she wanted to talk about me why didn't she say something that made sense? She told Bob I was jealous and maybe that was true, but I don't recall having any interest in Janie at all.

She was completely useless, she couldn't do anything except lay around and cry or chew on my mom or sleep. Even if I had washed my hands, she still couldn't play so what was I supposed to do with her? Mom kept asking me, "Don't you want to hold the baby?"

"No, thank you." I couldn't understand why everyone was so worked up about this kid.

The best thing they did was to keep her in a tiny crib in their own room so Debbie and I didn't have to put up with her yet.

I was thankful for that.

CHAPTER FIVE

The Property

Bob owned a small piece of property north of Sacramento in a little country town called Orangevale. When he first took us to see it, Janie had just been born, and Debbie and I overheard discussions about building a house big enough for our growing family.

Mom was really excited about a new house and sounded to me a little bit pushy about the plans, saying things like it needed to be built fast, because we were too crowded in the house she owned. The way she talked you'd think she and Bob were planning to have a bunch more kids right away.

We called it The Property. Bob got a Willy's Jeep Station Wagon that we loaded with tools from our garage and a bag full of snacks and drinks. It was about an hour's drive from our home on 52nd Street, and we spent at least one day each weekend there, and sometimes both days. It was two and a half acres of weeds and trees on a corner lot. There was an overgrowth of star thistle; weeds with yellow pointy stickers on blue-green stems. The land was so rich with topsoil that as long as it was damp, the noxious things could be pulled right out, but the thorns stuck in our clothes and tore our skin.

California poppies also grew wild, mostly on the banks of The Property that bordered Granite Avenue. They were fragile little things that wilted if you even got close to them with a shovel or a hoe. Debbie and I were warned that it was against the law to pick them, because they were the State Flower of California—after we had broken off a nice handful. The Property had some almond and olive trees in straight lines in what looked like an old orchard, along with blank spaces in between them, indicating trees that hadn't survived.

All the houses around The Property had fenced land with cows, chickens, dogs, and an occasional horse. Bob's brother lived at the end of the road about a mile away, and just beyond his property was a natural rock corral with towering oak trees that looked like they were million years old. A bunch of the larger flat granite boulders had grinding holes in them, and I discovered when it rained at Rock Corral, ants would bring up long-buried Indian beads made from bone. I had fun the weekends we went to The Property, and any time I got to spend in Rock Corral was nearly magical.

When they first mentioned building a house on The Property, I asked if we could have a dog and a horse.

"Yeah," Bob said, "There's room, and we'll have a few cows too. But there's a lot of work to do first."

I was on a mission from that moment on. New fruit trees were planted in the orchard to fill the rows where there were missing trees. Every weekend we pulled weeds, and when it was clear those efforts weren't keeping up with the regrowth, I was advanced to a weed sprayer that weighed almost as much as me.

Bob rented a trencher and we laid heavy plastic water lines across the orchard and I helped, holding the tape measure, doping the pipe ends with the purple thread sealing compound used to make the joined pipes leak proof. On weekends when there wasn't as much work to do, Debbie and I were told to water the new trees. It was a good job; it required sitting outside in the dirt, in the sun, but it had to be done in a particular way. We had to dig donut-shaped moats around the trees, and build up the borders to a certain height to hold the water. The water had to be turned on to a prescribed trickle so it would soak in really well. The speed had to be just right—not too slow because we didn't have all day but not too fast either or it would fill up fast and overflow.

I liked watering the trees, and we were educated and re-educated on the watering protocol, and when Bob was fairly certain we understood, he and Mom and Janie would leave us and go visit Bob's brother and his family down the street. We were supposed to water each tree for exactly thirty minutes, and that's a long time when you're a kid. Debbie and I would identify shapes in the clouds or get busy climbing trees or play cowboys and Indians or collect pretty quartz rocks or play with ladybugs or a million other things that were way more entertaining than watching water flow out of a hose. In-variably we got into trouble for not having all the trees watered when they got back or because the water would have broken its banks and flooded an area not intended to be wa-tered. But it wasn't too bad—Bob just yelled at us for a while and reminded us what a waste of space we were and how we couldn't do something that any monkey could be trained to do correctly. And the next weekend we'd do it again. Still, it was a nice way to spend a weekend and even better when we got it right.

In the summer when the work was done, Debbie and I were allowed to cross the street to pick the fat, sweet blackberries that grew on Mr. Rush's land. In the fall we laid tarps under the almond trees and collected the nuts into buckets. Some of the almonds produced bitter nuts that tasted bad, but others were sweet with soft shells that we could open with our hands. Mom learned to store them in a bunch of different ways—some were blanched with the skins off, some salted, and some roasted—and we were still left with lots and lots of raw almonds.

Finally, after the plans had been drawn up, the footprint of the house was staked out. Lines were drawn in the dirt to distinguish the various rooms and we all walked around going through imaginary walls as we went from room to room. Sure enough, Mom was pregnant again, and threatened aloud that the house better be ready before she had this baby. *Or what*, I remember thinking. Like she had any real threat up her sleeve.

It didn't take long to build the house once the carpenters finally got started. Even though he'd hired a contractor, it became a habit for Bob to find something wrong every time we went out to see the progress that had been made. His complaining was so routine that when one time he walked into the house and didn't say anything at all, Debbie blurted out automatically, "Oh my God.

When Bob asked what was wrong she said, "Nothing. I don't know, that's just what you always say."

The builders left nails and chunks of leftover wood everywhere and picking up after them was another job given to me and Debbie. We collected the nails in cans, and had to separate out the straight ones, and straighten the bent ones to reuse. We started a wood pile with the leftover wood pieces, after sorting the "fire" wood from the usable wood. Then, we were instructed to layer the usable wood pile, with the larger pieces on the bottom. Everything had to be done just so. Debbie and I helped Bob hang itchy and hot insulation in the interior walls of the house, something that the workers hadn't been paid to do. We started fencing the pasture after Bob bought an old tractor. And there was always brush to haul away. As the house progressed it seemed like we worked harder and harder.

It wasn't long before Bob started writing out "To Do" lists for Debbie and me. The lists were kind of fun in the beginning, it was like a personal note written to each of us. I tried hard to do everything on my list, but quickly discovered that the more I got done, the more work he added to my next list. After just a couple of weeks our lists were so long, we could never complete all the work he assigned and it stopped being fun.

It was a race to the finish, but Mom had the second baby in May, 1962, right before the house was completed. They named her Judy. I was nine years old then. We moved to The Property about a week later. It had been almost two years from the time we had started working on the place until we moved in, and there were still a lot of things we needed to do.

There were six olive trees around the front yard of our new house and three more in the pasture. I loved eating olives. I loved the big, juicy black ones with the hole in them that were served up in tiny bowls at Thanksgiving and sometimes Christmas.

But these weren't those kind of olives.

The olives on our trees were big and black all right, but they tasted bitter and hard and didn't have a nice tidy hole in them. Bob told me there was a Del Monte plant in town that would pay four dollars for a lug box full of olives right off the tree. I was very interested.

"What are lug boxes and where can I get some?" I asked, trying not to sound too excited. I didn't want my sisters to get in on the action.

The next day Bob picked up two of the boxes from Del Monte and when he unloaded them from the back of his truck, I saw that they were much larger than I had imagined. They were about three feet long, by two feet wide, and one foot deep. It was going to take a lot of olives to fill one. I shouldn't have worried that Debbie or Janie would want to get involved; they couldn't have been less interested.

I got a bucket and started collecting the good olives that had fallen on the ground. It was slow going. When I emptied my first bucketful into the box, it didn't even cover the bottom. It took me four days to fill the first box. By the end of the week, I had both the boxes filled. Bob loaded them into his truck and drove away, returning that night with my $8 and the two empty boxes. I was hooked. I filled them both again and in half the time, and asked Bob to bring back five boxes next time. I worked hard, and was amazed at the money I was able to make. I was the official olive picker in the house.

Business was good and the trees produced lots of olives, and I'd soon picked everything I could reach with a six-foot ladder. I got a three-legged semi-sturdy 25-foot ladder. It had a wide base, and the steps got narrower up at the top. The top step was about one foot square. The counter supporting third leg was attached by a hinge and was wobbly at best, but it gave me access to the olives higher up in the trees. I bought a smaller bucket to hold while I picked, and a larger bucket to attach to the side of the ladder.

One year, I got sick during the peak olive-picking season, and hired some of the kids from my street, paying them three dollars a box while I kept one dollar. That worked well but I discovered it's hard to find good help. Not everyone was as money hungry as me.

I realized, quite by accident, there was even bigger money to be made in loan sharking when my Mom asked to borrow three dollars to pay the paperboy. I was quite happy to loan her the money, at the going rate of six percent interest compounded daily. It was three weeks before she remembered to repay me. When I said she owed $4.69 including interest, I caught a bit of blow back. She didn't want to pay the inflated interest charge, but I told her business is business. She paid up but didn't turn into a repeat customer.

Regardless, I could definitely see an opportunity in money, and was always looking for ways to make more of it.

#

That fall Debbie and I were enrolled into the local Orangevale 4-H club, which at that time only had a few members.

4-H is an educational program, started in the 1890's, in every state in America. Its purpose was to teach country kids about agriculture. The organization expanded by the time we enrolled in September, 1962, to include nonagricultural subjects such as sewing, canning, and gardening. I wasn't interested in those things; I wanted to be in the horse group. Minor problem—I didn't have a horse and that was a somewhat obvious requirement. I argued that if 4-H was supposed to teach us about a particular subject, why did it only apply to kids who already owned the thing they wanted to learn about?

That wasn't the case with the sewing group. Those kids were going to make their projects. They didn't already have them. I guess I spouted off a couple of times too many as my argument backfired.

Mom enrolled me into the Sewing group. It was a dismal failure, and one not repeated. I had no indoor skills and was bored rigid with the girls in the sewing group. I only attended one or two meetings, then refused to go again and did not construct the required project.

I insisted I wanted an animal and would have been happy with the dog I'd always wanted, and I suppose partly to shut me up, they finally announced that they had bought a puppy. The next day Mom brought it home. Technically it was a dog, but in reality, it was a disgusting little turd that could barely breathe—a Pekingese Mom had already saddled with the hideous name Tinkerbelle. This was hardly the sturdy German Shepherd I had imagined would take off Bob's arm next time he hit me. No, this dog was about as frightening as a Kleenex tissue. I couldn't have been more disappointed.

Eventually, Bob bought a young Angus steer for me to raise for a 4-H Beef project. I named him Sonny, after Sonny Liston. I had listened to the fight between Liston and Cassius Clay on the radio on February 25, 1964, and had hoped Sonny would win. But when he didn't, I named the steer after him anyway, because I didn't like the big-mouthed Cassius.

The barn had only been started and the pasture wasn't completely fenced yet, so we tied the lead rope of Sonny's halter to one of the olive trees in the pasture. I was supposed to teach him to walk on a leash like a dog and brush him every day, so I could parade him around in my stupendously white 4-H jeans and button-down shirt the next spring at the County

Fair. The plan was for me to sell him at the fair for a zillion dollars. Of course, I didn't own Sonny, so I didn't expect to get any of that money.

Since Sonny was my 4-H project, it was my job to haul buckets of water, hay, and feed to him twice a day. The little shit would let me get just close enough to set the buckets down, and then he'd head butt me until I was out of his reach. Not the playful, "Oh isn't that cute," kind of head butt, this dude was like the real Sonny Liston, out to cause damage. He seriously stomped me into the ground a number of times. At ten years old, I weighed about 75 lbs., and it was all too obvious there was no way I was ever going to walk him anywhere. He was either mad about being tied up, or just plain mad in general. He lived the rest of his short, miserable life right there under that olive tree.

Then to my horror, Mom and Bob had him butchered, wrapped in white paper, and delivered into a big new freezer in our garage.

CHAPTER SIX

My Room

Debbie's and my room in the new house was painted titty pink and had wallpaper on two walls with tiny pink roses all over it. Nobody asked our opinion before they chose that color or paper. The room had two windows, one faced Granite Avenue and across the street was Mr. Rush's pasture with a creek running through it. Blackberry bushes grew wild, covering the creek in some spots.

In the cool, early mornings when the pasture looked empty, if I fixed my eyes just right, I saw it was really alive with pheasant and quail. Their feathers were the same color as the ground and weeds, and unless I stood very still and specifically looked for them, they were all but invisible. Sometimes they came into our yard to eat the fallen olives, but if they saw me move even when I was behind the window, they'd take flight in unison.

Mr. Rush ran cattle on his land and he had a big old Hereford bull who would stand in the corner nearest our bedroom and bellow loud as a truck horn announcing his presence. It was an ominous sound, since he was so big, but he never caused any real problem and soon I found it was easy to ignore his yelling.

Through the window on the other side of our room we could see the orchard and our barn. Once the barn was finished, we painted it dark red and trimmed around the doors in white.

The next thing we had to work on was fencing the orchard.

Bob had purchased the posts, and dipped the ends in creosote to keep them from rotting. They were stacked and waiting for me to paint the tops white. That was on the top of my To Do list that week.

After school I carried each of them over to the barn, leaned them at an angle against the barn wall, and painted them. After an hour or so they were dry and I restacked them so they were ready to plant around the orchard the following weekend.

It had been a lot of work, but I hadn't taken any shortcuts and was proud that I'd done a good job. It felt good to cross that big chore off my list. I cleaned the paint brush and put everything away, then went to my room. Judy crawled in to watch while I played with my plastic horses on the floor.

I heard Bob come home.

The first thing Bob always did when he got home was check our To Do lists to see what we had been doing. I heard the back door shut and knew he had probably gone out to inspect my work. Minutes later he appeared in the doorway of my room.

"What did you think you were doing?" he asked quietly.

"Well, I got all the posts painted and restack...." But he interrupted me.

"You painted the barn white," his voice was flat and accusing.

I looked up and saw the skin on his neck was red and prickly looking, and his eyes had gone empty again. I knew that look. But I had no idea what he was talking about. I briefly wondered if he was joking.

He reached down and lifted me off the floor by the neck of my favorite striped t-shirt, the one I wore nearly every day. I worried it was going to rip. He pulled me to my feet and held onto the front of my shirt when I felt a dull, hard slap on the side of my face and ear. My head spun so far to the right I remember seeing those little pink roses on the wall behind me, all in a blur.

"You weren't thinking were you? Huh, what'd you say?" He asked, baiting me, then slapped me again.

I knew better than to answer him; Debbie always argued back when she was getting hit and it was like pouring gas on a fire. I said nothing. I didn't resist. And I refused to cry. That was my only revenge, the only power I had; I wouldn't cry.

"You're a goddam dreamer," he said, still in a low, angry growl. "What were you thinking, huh?" And he hit me again, and again. I closed my eyes, the view was making me dizzy.

"You don't think, do you? You're always daydreaming," and another hard slap, "That's the problem, you *never* think." I heard Judy start to cry behind me. My head snapped back and forth with each hit.

I heard a noise in the hall and opened my eyes. I saw a flurry of movement behind Bob, someone coming into my room.

Thank God, I thought, *it's Mom, maybe she's going to hit him with something. A frying pan or a rock, something to make him stop.*

But she didn't hit Bob. She moved right past him, towards me, and then past me. Between slaps, I saw she had picked up Judy and held her tight against her chest. I watched the back of her head as she left the room. Bob kept asking questions he didn't want answered, and slapping me when he didn't get them.

My Mom. Our Mom. Why wouldn't she protect me from being beaten? I watched her walk away–carrying Judy. But there was nothing I could do, I was just a kid.

You'll survive, I told myself. *He'll stop when he gets tired.*

That's exactly what happened. Soon after Mom had gone, he let go of my shirt and left me standing in the middle of the room. I crawled onto my bed and curled into a tiny ball. When my breathing had quieted and my head stopped swimming, I slowly sat up. Gently, I pulled myself up to the window overlooking the orchard and barn.

The barn was as red as it had ever been.

Quietly, I crept outside to look. It was still red.

I stood right in front of the barn. Still red.

I *had* leaned the fence posts against it, to paint them white, but I'd been careful not to get any paint on the barn. I walked to the place I had been working and moved closer and closer toward the barn wall. With my nose about 12" away, I fixed my eyes like I was looking for quail, for something invisible.

Sure enough, there they were. A few tiny little flecks of white paint that had gotten onto the barn from the flicking of my paint brush.

CHAPTER SEVEN

The Therapist

"Your step-father was violent," she stated flatly.

"Yeah," I nodded.

"Did he drink? Was he an alcoholic?"

"No. He'd drink a beer now and then, but I never saw him drunk."

"So he was just mean?" she asked.

"Yeah." I nodded. "Well, he didn't like us, Debbie and me. We were in the way. But, yeah. He was a mean son of a bitch."

I thought about that for a minute. It was as fair an assessment as I could give him, probably better than he deserved. When I was little I had thought he was fairly normal for a step-parent. From movies I'd watched, he looked like an ordinary, garden variety Step-Monster. Back then, I had thought they were all like that.

CHAPTER EIGHT

Middle School

I began seventh grade as an eleven-year-old geek in a newly built school in Orangevale named Louis Pasteur Junior High School. I was five feet, eight inches tall, and weighed 89 pounds. I know this because the first day of school all students from both seventh and eighth grades were herded into the cafeteria like a bunch of sheep and were weighed and measured, and the data was recorded in our permanent files.

President Kennedy had been assassinated the year before, right before my birthday, and there was a lot of patriotic hype around keeping his Physical Fitness Program alive. I was mortified to be called out by the principal as the tallest and youngest student in our entire school. I imagine President Kennedy would have been mortified too if he knew that a girl built like a blade of grass was at the top of his esteemed fitness program. I was hardly physically fit. I could barely carry my own books.

As I left the gym, a little boy raced after me and asked my name. He said his name was Peanut, and I asked if he was old enough to be in school. He looked a lot younger than me.

"Yeah I'm old enough," he said, "I'm a midget. And you're a freak. We belong together." He smiled up at me sweetly. It turned out he was in some of the classes I was taking, and he suggested we be boyfriend and girlfriend. Peanut stood about three feet, eight inches tall.

"I don't know. What would we have to do?" I asked him.

"Just walk around together. Hold hands. That's all." He sounded like maybe he'd done that before. I marveled at his experience and confidence.

I agreed and we walked around between classes holding hands a few times. He was a tiny little guy with buzz-cut blonde hair that felt good when I touched it, and sky blue eyes. He was pretty smart too and had lots of friends. Peanut said sometimes we should eat lunch together so we did, and sometimes we worked on book reports together in the library.

On Halloween, he dressed up like a giant, wearing a rough burlap shirt stuffed with a pillow and a rope tied around his waist holding it up. I couldn't think of how to dress like a midget. I had outgrown nearly all my clothes over the summer, and was wearing Debbie's hand-me-down's to school, so my costume was a too-big dress, same as I wore every day.

Over the Christmas holiday, Peanut and his family moved to a different school district, and I never saw him again. I couldn't know it at the time, but Peanut would be the only boy I would hold hands with until I was sixteen years old.

I did well as a seventh grader. My favorite class was chemistry. My teacher had really bad body odor and big yellow stains under the arms of all his shirts, but when he started teaching us about the Periodic Table of the Elements, all that was forgotten. It was like a light came on inside me. It was a list of all the known elements, placed in the order of their atomic numbers starting with the lowest number. The elements were arranged into periods across the table, and grouped in columns. Elements in a group have electrons arranged in similar ways, which gives them similar chemical properties, and they can be counted on to behave in similar ways. There was such symmetry and beauty in the way the table was constructed.

The colors of the elements had different meanings too, the ones in blue are gases, greens are liquids, and blacks are solids. And even the border of each box is significant. It was the most brilliant thing I'd ever seen.

I couldn't believe the other kids weren't as excited about this amazing piece of information. It was like discovering a massive Easter egg filled with secrets and peeling it back layer by layer, and each layer revealed something new and incredible. I was in awe. I stared at that table for hours, afraid if I looked away I would lose the magic of the mysteries it held.

It was an elegant revelation. I can't recall being so excited about anything else during my school years.

Except sex education.

That was a world-shattering bit of information. Seventh grade girls were sent into a room to watch a movie that showed pictures of naked boys and girls, which was shocking enough. Then in time lapse photography, breasts, penises, and hair sprung out all over them. In full color it graphically depicted how a baby is made in a petri dish, under a microscope, and how aggressively the sperm raced to get to the blob in the dish.

The film also talked about condoms, and a skinny woman demonstrated how to put one on a banana. I didn't think I could ever be more embarrassed. I couldn't look at anyone, and I couldn't look away.

I was horrified.

At home, I told Mom about the film I'd seen and asked her about that petri dish and how could it grow a baby. She fussed and fumed and told me to go to bed.

Instead of giving up, I became obsessed with the subject. I went to the library at lunchtime and tried looking up the new words in the index card file. Every time I got near the SEX cards someone always walked past me and I had to slam the drawer shut. After several failed tries, I finally got the first few digits of the source code and wandered into that aisle of the library. Most were science books, and after selecting one, I was elated to find the word sex in the glossary. On the page mentioned, there were colored pictures of flaccid penises with every style of infection and disease you could imagine, and for years I thought every man housed a sick penis of one variety or another in their pants. I couldn't make eye contact with any man for weeks.

But that wasn't the information I was after.

Next I located a book called *The Sex Life of Youth,* which sounded more likely to be what I was looking for. It had a huge section on the dangers of petting, a new word which had not been discussed in the film, but there were no pictures or actual descriptions of what petting was so I discarded that information as not useful. I flipped the pages and found some black-and-white photos of fallopian tubes. Again, no help. Everything was so vague.

Finally I gave up and went back to Mom and demanded answers. She promised she'd get me some information. A day or two later she handed me an old dog-eared book from the County Library, full of illustrated pictures depicting how a baby is made (not in a petri dish) and what it looks like each month as it gestates. There were pencil sketches of naked boys and girls, and I studied the whole thing cover to cover like it was the lost book of Nostradamus.

The downside of my research was that I thought everyone could tell just by looking at me that I had just read these books and looked at these pictures and knew that this was all I could think about. And if they had thought so, they would have been right.

Thank God for girlfriends. I picked up most of what I needed to know by lingering between classes in the girls' restroom. Those girls had the low-down on everything. But most helpful of all were the several conversations I had with my friend Linda, whose older sister had already had a baby. She filled in enough of the remaining blanks, and I finally felt like I had the whole picture.

Linda was a font of information. She even knew what all the nasty words meant, and used them with flair and proficiency. Linda was an awesome friend.

#

I made the Cheerleading Squad that year. I don't know how–I couldn't have been any more uncoordinated. But I tried out and with enough pity votes I made it. I got to wear my cute cheerleader skirt to school on game days, and I rejoiced in my newfound popularity. It was the first time I had a lot of friends at school. I had to go to practice twice a week, which helped me correct my slumpy posture and flailing limbs.

But problems started almost immediately. Mom was driving me to and from the practices and Bob didn't like that. I was told I would have to find a ride with someone else, and it couldn't be a teenager–as if teenage boys were lined up around the block just waiting to drive me somewhere. Fortunately, the school was only a couple of miles away and I could ride my bike.

Bob said the cheerleader outfit was extravagant and outside the budget, but Mom had already purchased it for me. Then, suddenly Bob became suspicious of every practice and game I attended. Without telling me, he and Mom came to one of the games and watched from a distance, never letting me know they were there.

Afterward, I was excited to learn they had watched me cheer, but then they said I had embarrassed them terribly, and had acted childishly.

They said my popularity and looks would get me knocked up, and that I'd run around with all sorts of boys, and drink and embarrass the entire family. I was really getting tired of hearing about all the horrible things I might do. I was eleven years old. How did they get from cheerleading to pregnancy?

"Were you a cheerleader?" I asked Mom.

"No," she answered, then looked at me quizzically. "Why do you ask?"

"Because you have four kids," I pointed out, expecting her to follow my logic.

She stared at me with a sad look like I had just lost my mind.

"Never mind," I sighed and rolled my eyes. It seemed to be the only reasonable response.

A couple of days later, Debbie and I missed the school bus. We could have caught it, but Mom kept giving us one more thing to do before we could leave, and before we knew it the bus was rounding the corner and heading off down the street. Mom said she would drive us to school. As we pulled up in front of the school, she started to cry and Debbie asked her what was wrong. With her face in her hands Mom blubbered that she and Bob were getting divorced.

I thought a divorce sounded pretty good right about then, and I didn't want to listen to her carry on about how sad she was, so I hopped out of the car and hurried to my class. As usual, Debbie stayed in the car and talked with Mom.

The following day, Mom happily announced that she and Bob would not be divorcing after all. But, she said, we would all have to make some sacrifices and that would include each of us giving up something important to us. She had decided I would give up cheerleading.

I didn't ask what she had to give up. Brains and the ability to reason had evidently been on the chopping block along with ruining my life. I pretended I didn't care and once I was out of earshot, I made good use of a couple of the words Linda had taught me.

CHAPTER NINE

Red

I got twenty dollars in the mail from my grandparents for my thirteenth birthday. I kept all my money in a Karo Syrup screw top jar, with a picture of Black Beauty taped around it, under my bed. Every time I added money to the jar, I dumped out the contents and counted it all. I found it very motivating to see the balance increase, even if just by a little. This time I had a total of $125, plus change. I thought it might be enough to buy a horse. But I also remembered the promise Bob had made on the day he and Mom got married. He had said he would adopt Debbie and me on my thirteenth birthday, and I wondered if the money might help pay for the adoption. I decided I would offer it to Bob when he brought up the subject.

I waited all day for Bob to say something about it. Finally, when it was almost bedtime, I asked him if we could talk in private. We went into my bedroom.

He sat on my bed with his back to the wall with the pink roses. I asked if he was still going to adopt us like he had said he would.

He sucked in a deep breath then sighed and said, "No."

He cocked his head and rolled his lips inward, then just looked at me. I could tell he hadn't forgotten but he obviously wished that I had.

"It's not a good business decision," he finally said, and looked me square in the eyes. "You understand?"

I looked down and studied my feet. I had sort of anticipated this, since he hadn't brought it up himself. But how in hell was this a business decision?

No, I thought angrily, *I don't understand. What's to understand? A promise is a promise and not keeping one makes you a liar. A big, fat, ugly liar.*

And now that Debbie and I had changed our names to his for the last seven years of our lives—more than half my life—what were we supposed to do with that? Didn't that make us liars too? There was nothing I wanted to say out loud, and after a few minutes he got up and walked out.

We never spoke about it again.

Well, I thought, *I guess I have $125 to spend on a horse.* I started checking the classifieds and circling any ads for horses in my price range. Mom asked what I was doing, and after I explained, she advised I needed to ask Bob first. That irritated me a little because he had already said The Property was big enough for a dog and a horse, the pasture was fenced with cows in it, and we even had a barn with two horse stalls. More to the point, I was the one who took care of all the feeding, cleaning, and everything related to the animals. Why did I have to ask him again? It felt like begging.

But the next day after breakfast, I did ask. I told him how much money I had saved, and outlined how much I could expect to make as I continued doing my various lawn-mowing, babysitting, and olive-picking jobs in order to pay for horse feed. Once I'd made my case, I didn't say any more. I let him think. Every second that ticked by without him saying no seemed like a victory. I wondered if he would say a horse wasn't a good business deal, which I knew it wasn't, but I had wanted one for so long, it wasn't business sense that was driving me. I wanted Bob to say yes about this. I needed him to say yes about something. I sat looking at my hands folded in my lap and counted off the seconds in my head. *One one-thousand, two one-thousand, three one-thousand...*

I waited for him to clear his throat, say something, anything.

"Yeah, I don't care if you buy a horse," he finally said. Just like that. As casually as if he'd said, "Gosh, isn't the sky blue." *"I don't care if you buy a horse."*

"Really?" I asked, "Really? Thank you, oh wow, thank you." I could barely believe I'd heard right, the oracle had spoken; I could really have a horse.

But the moment had passed and he had buried his head back into the newspaper.

I ran out of the kitchen and straight into Debbie and shouted, "I get to buy a horse! Bob said I can have a horse!" I was still leaping around when I told Mom the news. She immediately verified the decision with Bob, making sure I had understood him correctly, then she and I sat down and together we searched the classified ads.

We spent the next few weekends locating horses that were nearby The Property and were for sale within the $100 range. There weren't very many, but I was allowed to call and inquire about each one. The first horse sounded promising but turned out to be chronically lame and the owner said he'd been severely foundered. Another was a retired race horse the owner called a "companion horse," which I learned meant it was really old and not fit to ride. They were just looking for a home for it, like an old folk's home.

Then, as so often happens when you're looking for one thing and find something else, I found two different colts advertised for $100 each. They were both weaned and sounded healthy. Mom drove me to see the first one, a colt named Happy who was owned by a Mexican family. Happy was very friendly and followed us around the yard like a big dog. Unfortunately he was horribly malnourished with a painfully ugly, swollen belly and badly shaped hooves. He was very sweet though, and I hated to drive away and leave him there, but Mom said we needed to talk about it. She convinced me to hold off making a decision until I'd seen the other colt.

I'd spoken to a woman on the phone about the second one, and when we pulled up in front of her house I was sure we were at the wrong address. Every foot of the front lawn was covered in big plywood cutout yard art, the kind that looks like a fat woman's bottom in the air. I couldn't see a horse barn anywhere.

When she came out of her house, the woman said her husband made the big cutouts and they were for sale if we were interested. We were not.

"She's a beautiful golden palomino filly—a little over a year old. And she ain't got no name yet. You get to name her yourself," the woman announced a bit too sure of herself.

She led us through an unmown back yard littered with odd bits of trash and past an empty, broken above-ground swimming pool. I could see a corral behind the pool that looked like it had been constructed that same day out of old pallets and held together with bailing wire. In it was the filly.

The old woman was right. This was a beautiful filly. Slick-coated, healthy-looking, and as wild and crazy as a mountain goat full of ticks. That filly ran around her makeshift corral, as if the devil was chasing her, her eyes wide and nostrils flared. She never once slowed down or stopped to look at us. As we got closer she crashed head first into the boards. I backed away from the fence, not wanting to scare her.

"She just needs gentling down," the old woman claimed.

My heart sunk as we watched her race around inside her pen, then Mom told the woman we would think about it.

"Well, don't wait too long," the woman hollered as she watched us pick our way through the yard and back toward our car, "there's somebody else looking at her."

Yeah, I'll bet, I thought. I had only ridden a couple of horses in my lifetime, but I was smart enough to realize I was not equipped to provide what this horse needed, no matter how pretty she was.

Mom must have said something to Bob about my dismal attempts to find a horse, because the next day he announced he knew a guy at work named Gene, who was a horse guru, and he had asked Gene to help me find a good one. I was still thinking about Happy and the palomino filly and really didn't want to clutter up my decision-making process even further, but I thanked him anyway.

About a week later, Gene called our house and asked to speak to me. That was odd—a grown man wanting to talk to me on the telephone. I had expected he would talk to Bob since they were friends, or even Mom.

But I took the phone and listened while he said he had located a nice, well-bred, healthy, eighteen-month-old colt and wanted me to go look at it that very day. I handed the phone to Mom, who worked out the details.

Gene picked me up about an hour later and drove me out to a real horse farm, with green grass and a proper barn. There were several healthy-looking horses in the pasture. He parted the barbed wire fence between two posts and held them so I could duck in between. A red horse with a single white star and stripe on his forehead trotted up to us. He was about 14 hands, and stuck his neck out to sniff Gene's pockets. It struck me that the red colt seemed to know Gene, and I wondered if Gene owned these horses and maybe even this farm. He kept talking and said the colt was a full-blooded quarter horse, with Red Dog on his father's side and out of a Texas Dandy mare, terms that meant nothing to me, but sounded good. The colt was well muscled and his feet looked in good shape. We walked around a little, and as the colt followed us I noticed he moved well and didn't appear lame or tender in any way. Best of all, he had the kindest eyes of any horse I'd ever seen. He was perfect.

"The only problem is he's a little more expensive than what you've been talking about," Gene said.

I felt a boulder hit the bottom of my stomach. Damn it, there was always a catch.

"How much," I asked, and cringed while I waited for the answer.

"They want $125 for him and that's really a bargain. They could easily get more than that if they took him to auction."

I explained that $125 was every cent I had, and I couldn't buy him for that because I needed some cash to buy hay and feed. No, I said to his next question, my stepdad would not buy his feed. I was sure it wasn't a possibility. I turned away from the colt and walked quickly back to Gene's truck, angry with him for even bringing me out there.

He drove me home in silence.

The next weekend, Gene called again and asked to speak to me. "Are you ready for me to bring that red colt to you?" he asked.

I was instantly angry. Don't you DARE, I wanted to scream.

"No, I don't have any more money than I did last weekend. I haven't had a chance to earn any more yet."

"Well, I got a surprise for ya," he drawled. "I got him for $115." He waited for me to say something, and when I didn't he continued, "So I've got him loaded in the trailer, I'll bring him on over to your place in about thirty minutes, okay?"

I didn't speak. I was mentally calculating how much feed I could buy with ten dollars and how soon I could make more money.

"Aw right then, see you soon," he said, and hung up.

I felt as near to dread as I'd ever felt. This was happening way too fast, and knowing how systematic Bob was, this was not going to go over well. I had learned not to spring things on Bob, it always set him off. I was terrified.

I hung up the phone. I turned and looked at my family sitting around the kitchen table still eating breakfast, and told them in a small voice, "I think I just bought a horse."

Debbie and Janie cheered. Mom wanted to know what Gene had said, and Bob continued reading his newspaper as if I hadn't said anything. I was slightly comforted he hadn't blown up immediately, and reasoned if he had changed his mind or was mad about this he wouldn't let Gene unload the colt from his trailer. The hard part for me was over. I happily told all of them the deal Gene had made getting the price reduced. Bob still hadn't spoken and again, I decided if he had any issues, he'd take them up with Gene.

I got my Karo Syrup jar from under my bed and counted out my money. After putting $115 in my right front pocket, and the extra ten dollars in my left front pocket, I went outside to wait.

I recognized Gene's truck as it came down the road and past the trees at Phillips's place. Sure enough, he was pulling a trailer. It was so surreal knowing that the red colt I'd just seen was inside the trailer coming toward me. I had dreamed about this day for so long and now it was actually happening.

Gene pulled up in front of our house and before he opened his truck door, everyone piled out of the front door. Debbie and Janie joined me at the side of the road, Mom held Judy, and then even Bob came out. He still hadn't said anything. I searched his face, then relaxed when I saw a little bit of a smile. This was going to be okay.

Gene opened the horse trailer and Red backed out in a very gentlemanly fashion. I was proud of him for being so well mannered. Wearing a cotton halter and lead rope he followed Gene as he brought him to me. When Gene handed me the lead rope, Red nuzzled my pockets and I remembered my money. Everyone was smiling and said how pretty Red was as I handed Gene my hard-earned $115.

I jumped when Gene leaned in toward me. But he just whispered, "I paid $125, but I wanted you to have him. That's my gift to you."

I could have cried. I thanked him, and as he closed up the trailer he said, "That halter and lead rope are yours too. Just take good care of him."

I thanked him again and he got back into his truck. It struck me as odd Bob didn't shake Gene's hand, or thank him, or invite him into the house for a cup of coffee. In fact, Bob acted like he didn't even know Gene. But I didn't spend too much time thinking about it. I had the most gorgeous, sweetest horse standing right in front of me and he was mine.

Gene waved good bye and drove away in his truck, the empty trailer bouncing along behind.

As I watched the dust swirl in the truck's wake, I heard Bob's voice behind me.

"What are you going to do with him?" he asked.

"Well, he's too young to ride yet, I'll just…"

"No," Bob interrupted. He was smiling. "I mean, where are you going to keep him?"

I was still happily chirping away, "In the pasture of course. Well, maybe in the horse stall sometimes when it's hot or the weather…"

Bob interrupted again. "No," shaking his head, and smiling that same little smile. "No. I said you could buy a horse. I *never* said you could keep it here."

I couldn't believe what he had said. Time stopped as the reality of that sentence hit me like a wrecking ball. I spun around and stared at Bob, his words hanging in the air between us. Then I turned around and looked back down the road and could still see some of the dust floating in the air that Gene's truck had kicked up. I stared at it as if I could somehow send him a signal to come back and put the red colt back into the trailer–reverse time–and make everything the way it had been just minutes before. But he was out of sight, and I had no way to call him back. I didn't even know his phone number, and I already knew I wouldn't give Bob the satisfaction of asking for it.

I turned back to face Bob. "What...what am I supposed to do?" My voice quivered, and I hated myself for feeling helpless, fighting back the threat of tears, realizing he had trapped me, and all of it turning instantly to anger when he answered.

Still smiling that incessant, gloating smile he answered lightly, "I don't care what you do. But don't come home until you've gotten rid of him."

With that, he turned away and calmly walked back into our house with my mother trailing close behind. My sisters reluctantly followed them.

I stood blinking back tears, a thirteen-year-old girl on the side of the road holding a lead rope attached to the most beautiful horse I could ever have imagined, ten dollars in my pocket, and nowhere to go.

I wanted to get away from there as fast as I could. I turned down Granite Avenue and walked away from The Property, the red colt at my side. The old man in the little house next to us didn't have any land, and the people next door to him had about eight kids but no animals so I kept walking. Mr. Dimali was an old Italian man who owned property on the next block. He had cattle and a horse named Zip, so I stopped and asked if I could rent pasture from him. He said no and shut the door in my face. I asked at every home we came across that had property attached, first just trying to rent pasture, then as the day wore on, just trying to give the red colt away. Not many people were home, and those that were, didn't want a horse to take care of.

We walked a long distance. After several hours we were well out of the area I was familiar with, and I was tired and thirsty. Red's head hung lower and lower as the day wore on. But we kept walking, and we stopped at every home that looked like it had space to keep a horse. Everyone was quick to answer, and the answer was always no.

It was warm out, but not hot. Even so, I worried that I needed to find water for Red and me, because my throat was dry and I had no idea when Red had last had a drink. The sun was getting lower in the sky, and our feet were dragging. I tried to think of something else to do with the colt, but nothing came to me except to keep trying. Finding my way home was beginning to concern me too, as it would be dark in a couple more hours and I really didn't know where we were.

We arrived at a T-junction and stopped while I decided which way to go. To continue straight would take us over a rise and I had no idea if there were any houses beyond that hill. If we turned, the road dipped down before it leveled out, but there were only a couple of homes in sight. We went straight.

Just over the rise I could see a newish home with a paddock-sized pasture next to a large hay barn. There was nothing in the pasture. As we got closer I could see a bunch of kids playing around the house, and a man in the driveway, working on an upside-down bicycle. The house was set back a little way off the street, so the man noticed Red and me when we turned into his driveway. He stood and watched us approach.

I got nervous the closer we got. I decided if he said no, I would at least ask him for water. The man didn't speak until we were right in front of him.

"Hello," he said, and took off his ball cap. His features were scrunched up because he was looking into the setting sun.

"Um, I was wondering, uh…would you like a horse? I mean, for your kids?" My voice wavered. I didn't really want to give the colt away, but I was running out of options and figured I'd better start with my best offer and see what happened. The man just stood looking at me with his face wrinkled up so I tried again.

"I, uh…I just bought this colt and um, well, I can't keep him, and you have all these *kids,* and that pasture and I thought, they, they might would, uh, course he's not broke yet but, uh, excuse me, do you have any water?" My mouth was so dry it felt like the words were all sticking together and I couldn't get them out. I felt like I was crying inside but was so dry there weren't any tears. My throat choked up, and I suddenly HAD to sit down, and my knees were crumpling. "Could I…could I please…"

"Hey, hey, hey, sit down, sit down, sit down," he said as he rushed to pull over a lawn chair and I sat. "I'll be right back, don't go anywhere," he said and in three steps he was inside his house.

I wasn't going anywhere.

He came back out with his wife who handed me a big glass of water. I drank sloppily, which embarrassed me, but I couldn't help it. My hand shook and water sloshed all over my shirt as I drank in big gulps, then coughed, then I immediately felt guilty about not first taking care of Red. I started to pour some of the water into my hand for the colt, but was stopped.

"No, no, no, no, no, I'll take care of him. You drink your water," the man said and took the lead rope from me and led the colt away. It didn't even occur to me to go with him.

When the man came back, I asked if Red was able to get some water. "Yeah, he's fine," he said. Then I saw Red standing in the pasture, in the shadow of the barn, and I took in a deep breath and blew it out, shaking off the weight of my nerves. Red was in a pasture.

"Now," the man said. "Tell us what's going on."

I told them, starting with how I'd saved enough money to buy a horse, then Gene found this one, but he was too much money, but he delivered him anyway, and what Bob had said.

At that point the man's wife covered her mouth and hurried inside their house. When she came back she brought a sandwich that I ate in just a couple of bites, then realized it might not have been for me. I apologized, but she said no, she'd meant for me to eat it. I thanked her, then continued, telling them where I had been with the colt and that I really didn't have a plan, but I had to find someplace to leave him, and that I had $10 left over to pay for feed or rent pasture and how I could get more because I had lots of jobs and if they wouldn't mind very much I thought he was a good horse with good manners and...I stopped because the words hung up in my throat.

They didn't say anything.

Then, for the second time that day, I asked if they wanted a horse for their kids, because clearly, I couldn't keep him, and I would be willing to just give him to them.

They looked at each other for a moment, then the man nodded and spoke. "You can keep him here for a month, he'll be fine in that pasture, and we'll see if things don't work out for you at home."

I pulled the sweaty ten dollar bill out of my pocket, "Here, use this to buy him some…"

"You keep that," he interrupted gruffly. "We've got feed. He'll be fine."

It was nearly dark, and the woman began gathering up her kids and telling them to get into the house. The man asked me where I lived. I looked around, but wasn't sure where I was.

"You know your address, don't you?" he asked. "Get in the car. I'll drive you home."

I was breaking one of the hard and fast rules: never accept a ride with a stranger, but this man was definitely not a teenager and he had my horse so he wasn't really a stranger and besides, I was so tired I really didn't care. I must have slept part of the way back, because suddenly we were in front of my house.

"Is this it?" he asked.

"Yes," I said, and thanked him again, then leapt out of the car and quickly went inside. Nobody spoke to me. It was like I was invisible. Dinner was already over and I quietly went into the bathroom and took a bath, then went straight to bed.

Nobody in my family ever asked me where I had left the colt. It was as if he'd never existed.

That was the start of my personal philosophy to not care too much about anything. If they didn't know what I wanted, they couldn't hurt me with it. And, I would do everything I could not to be noticed.

Being invisible had its advantages.

CHAPTER TEN

The Therapist

"Where was your biological father when all this was going on?" she asked. "Did you ever try to call him?"

"I never saw him after our mom remarried. He had his own family."

"*You* were also his family," she pointed out.

I shrugged. "He paid his child support. I guess he felt like that was his only obligation."

She shook her head and looked away.

After a few seconds she turned back.

"Go on."

CHAPTER ELEVEN

Red – Part II

I was still no closer to finding a place to keep Red when my thirty days were up. I had earned a few more dollars babysitting a neighbor's three little boys, and weeding some garden beds, and I'd gotten a little more cash from my grandparents for Christmas. The new total in my Karo bottle was close to thirty-five dollars. I put the money in my pocket and set off on my bicycle. I wasn't even sure I could find the house again. It was a month since I'd been there, and I had slept while the man had driven me back home. There was nothing to do but try, I thought. I decided the worst thing that could happen would be if I never found the place and he kept the colt, a consequence I was prepared to accept.

I tracked the way I'd gone that day to the best of my memory, and took one or two wrong turns, but figured out my mistakes soon enough. I arrived at his house after riding hard for about ninety minutes. Riding my bike made the trip much faster.

Red was in the pasture, fat and hairy. He looked bigger, like he'd grown taller. The man was in his garage sitting on a stool in front of a workbench. He turned and watched me ride into his driveway.

"I still don't have any place to keep him," I blurted out, short of breath, then waited for him to speak.

"Your stepdad hasn't changed his mind?" he asked as he stood to talk with me.

"No. He's not going to."

"Well, your horse isn't causing any trouble and he's doing a good job on that grass. Let's give it another month and see where we're at. I've got some ideas I'm working on," he took off his ball cap and scratched his head while he talked. I offered him the money I'd brought, but again he refused it and said the colt was doing fine.

I stayed and brushed Red, told him why I hadn't come to see him until now, and hung around the barn as long as I thought I could without being considered a pest, then I got my bike and rode back home.

It was the last week of January, and it was cold if you stood still very long.

Thirty days later I was back, and again I told the man that nothing had changed.

This time the man said he had an idea he wanted to talk over with me. He said he'd done some work for an old guy who lived over by me, a Mr. Rush, and asked if I knew him.

Of course I did.

"Well," the man said, "He has agreed to let me use the corner of his pasture in exchange for some work I did for him. It's a triangle piece of property, with a swampy run-off creek running through the middle of it, but it's attached to an old barn so your horse could get out of the weather. I fixed the fence around it. Do you think that would work for you?"

I knew the exact corner he was talking about and it was perfect. "Oh my gosh, are you serious?" I said. "I've got money I can pay him now, and I can..."

"Quit trying to give your money away," he laughed. "Keep it for oats and hay. There's no rent on this pasture, it's all taken care of," he beamed.

I walked Red back over to Mr. Rush's place, and the man was already waiting there in his car with my bicycle by the time we arrived. We introduced Red to his new pasture and I checked the water tank then cleaned the barn of cobwebs. It was perfect, and I kept saying so.

"Just promise me you'll stay in school and not get into trouble," he said. "That's the only thing you've got to do. And take care of your horse."

Fabulous. Apparently, everyone was certain I was going to get knocked up. But I promised him I'd stay out of trouble, and I thanked him again. It seemed like such an easy promise to make.

It had been the most exceptional day. I lingered as long as I dared, then I rode my bike home.

#

Rules were changed to allow me twenty minutes each day to get to Red's pasture, feed him, and get home. If I pedaled like a crazy person I could spend a few minutes brushing him.

Mom bragged, "Kathi spends every spare moment with that colt," which was true in one sense, but incredibly misleading in another. I still had a long To Do list that kept me extremely busy. The only time I found to spend with Red was early in the mornings. I got up and out of the house before anyone else woke and could safely spend an hour or so brushing him and fussing with his feet or laying a burlap sack across his back while he ate, to get him used to having weight on him. Then I'd have to hurry back home to feed our cows and chickens and be in the house to get ready for school.

When I decided Red was old enough to be castrated, I called one of the two veterinarians in town. I was upset that he hobbled Red and threw him to the ground, and was even more horrified when I saw two of the neighborhood kids looking out from Mr. Rush's window. I stopped the veterinarian and said I didn't want him to do it. He got angry with me and said so. But I'd made up my mind, so he untied Red and left without charging me a dime.

I called the other veterinarian and explained on the phone that I wanted Red sedated, not thrown down like some rodeo calf, and he agreed to do it that way. It was done the next weekend without anyone else looking on–which I was grateful for.

Mom told everyone that I fired the first vet because I wanted to assist him with the castration and he wouldn't let me. That wasn't true at all. I wished it had been done before I even bought Red, and I wanted nothing to do with the actual procedure. But it was necessary, and since I was paying for it I wanted it done humanely. Mom's insistence on her version of the events seemed raunchy and sick. What she said disgusted me.

After Red was two years old and strong enough, I gradually started leaning across his back while he ate and finally, I put all my 100 pounds on him. He never even flinched. Over the next few weeks I gradually climbed up onto his back. I only had his cotton halter but I could ride him around his pasture bareback. Soon I was taking him out into Mr. Rush's big pasture and rode like an Indian, down low and clinging tight around his neck as he ran up and down the hills. It was pure joy—until we came to the creek. Red suddenly put on the brakes and I did a flying Wallenda over his head.

For a colt that had spent the last few months living in a swampy pasture, Red was loath to get his feet wet. Try as I might, I could never coax him to cross the creek even at the most shallow spot. We stayed on dry ground after that.

I gained access to Rock Corral and pretended I really was an Indian riding under the ancient oak trees and around the big, smooth granite boulders. Red proved to be a true Indian pony and would go where I wanted without even a halter, just responding to my leg pressure. He never ran off, and he never bucked. He was a true gentleman.

CHAPTER TWELVE

Cow Pie High

It was September, 1966, when I started classes at Casa Roble High School, or Cow Pie High as I preferred to call it, due to it being built smack in the middle of a cow pasture. Inflation in the US grew to fund the Vietnam War. The hotly contested Space Race to get a man on the moon was a topic of discussion. Race riots were in the news. London was leading fashion with patterned pants and flowered shirts, knee-high boots, short skirts, and vinyl hats. The Beatles had just played in Candlestick Park in San Francisco, and lots of kids around me were talking about it.

I started the school year with five dresses my grandmother had lovingly made for me over the summer. They were all sewn from the same pattern, from five different pieces of cotton cloth. One had a bit of leftover lace as a collar, two had short sleeves, and three of them were sleeveless. Debbie got exactly the same dresses, just a size larger. We had one dress for each day of the week.

Along with the dresses, we each got a pair of shoes that had to last the entire year. I had begged for tennis shoes but was told they weren't good value and wouldn't hold up. Instead, Mom bought a pair of moss green Hush Puppie flats for me to wear all year. Those shoes, unfortunately, held up remarkably well.

Mom cut my hair even shorter. The style was straight and long. My hair was naturally curly, and she thought she was cutting my wet bangs in a straight line. But when they dried, it looked as if a drunken monkey had been at them.

As I surveyed myself in the mirror I realized the only thing I had going for me was straight teeth.

Because we lived so close to the school, we couldn't ride a school bus anymore. We would walk to and from, as it was only about half a mile from The Property. The school occupied the corner lot at the opposite end of the street from Bob's brother's house. But, because we weren't supervised, new rules were initiated. Lots of new rules.

Classes let out at 2:45 in the afternoon, and we were given until 3:05 to be inside the house and calling Mom at work to verify our arrival.

We weren't allowed to wear makeup. It was a totally unnecessary rule for me because I didn't have any makeup and I wouldn't have known what to do with it if I had. Nonetheless, I was outraged, as if THAT would have fixed my entire ensemble.

We weren't allowed to wear skirts above the middle of our knees. That was painful, as miniskirts were the style. We couldn't wear nylon stockings, nor talk to boys, nor talk on the telephone, as apparently we had plenty of time to talk to our friends during school. We weren't allowed to bring anyone inside the house, nor anyone even at the house without proper permission as this would distract us from doing our chores. Of course, all rules only applied to Debbie and me.

Janie and Judy were now in elementary school and had no rules. But they were little kids. I was especially amused that we were forbidden to date until we were sixteen years old. I looked like a sexually confused boy. Nobody even tried to talk to me. Nevertheless I started high school fully prepared for all the boys to flock around, and I was ready to reject every single date they offered.

In addition to the universal rule of never getting into a car with strangers or teenagers, now we were also strictly forbidden to ride in a car driven by anyone under the age of twenty-one, at any time for any reason. Nobody I knew had a car so this rule wasn't one I worried about. Joyriding had never occurred to me.

But what about ambulance drivers, I wondered, and policemen, are they over twenty-one? And bus drivers. Would I need to see some identification before boarding a bus?

I still had twenty minutes in the evening to ride my bike down to feed Red and get back home. In the mornings, I just had to be home in time to do my chores and get to school. I was responsible for all the outside chores, which included feeding the animals morning and night, changing the water pipes in the pasture every twenty minutes after school, cleaning the barn and chicken coop, watering the trees in the orchard, weeding and mowing the yard on the weekends, washing both the cars once a week, and emptying all the trash, and after separating it, burning the paper products. Other outside chores were added to my list whenever they thought of a new one.

Debbie had all the inside chores including cooking, laundry, and cleaning. And we both washed up the dinner dishes.

Automatic dishwashers weren't "good value," because "they had us," the human dishwashers.

When he got bored, Bob liked to inspect every dish, bowl, and pan in the kitchen cupboards, and if any of them were found with one single dirty speck, everything was dragged out of the cupboards and we had to wash all of them again.

On weekends, in addition to our everyday chores we had long To Do Lists, with more items than could ever be completed, and never were. Any item that didn't get done was rolled to the top of next week's To Do List. Bob really enjoyed writing up our lists.

All the lists and rules and chores were exhausting, and I couldn't wait to see what they would add next.

My guess was they tried to keep us so busy and ugly that we wouldn't have the opportunity to meet or talk with any of the horrible boys who they thought were intent on knocking us up. I wondered what awful things Bob had done when he was in high school to be so concerned about what Debbie or I might do.

To enforce his rules, Bob made unscheduled visits to our high school. We were called out of class so he could make sure our skirts were long enough, inspect us for make-up, and at the same time check our files for possible forged sick notes. I had never thought of forging a sick note until Bob said he was checking for them. What a novel idea.

While crafting their rules, they forgot about after-school activities, so when Debbie actually landed a part in the school play, they had to add that to the list of things we couldn't do. We weren't allowed to participate in any after-school activities, no sports, no clubs, nor even watch games or go to dances, nothing. Debbie was told to decline the part she'd won in the play. She was rightfully upset and let everyone know about it, arguing loudly that it wasn't fair. We were told we had plenty of chores to do at home, we didn't have time for that sort of nonsense, and (of course) it would only end up with us drunk and pregnant.

That was Mom and Bob's biggest worry—woe be the one to bring shame upon our righteously tight-knit and upstanding family, and certainly it would be Debbie or Kathi, the harlot sluts they'd been burdened with raising. I think if we had been Catholic, we would have certainly been deposited in a convent long before we had gotten to high school.

My grades that first year were still pretty good—B's and a couple of C's. I took a business machines class and excelled at typing, burning down the house with a seventy-five word per minute pace. The school also had an old adding machine I learned to use by touch, but that was the extent of the business machines we had back in 1966.

I took Spanish, and was delighted to find a Japanese woman teaching the class. I learned a minimal amount of the language, and after two full years of it, could do a reasonable job of ordering from the Taco Bell menu, but badly embarrassed myself saying anything else in Spanish.

I also took Journalism as an elective, and that was my favorite class. I discovered I loved it and fancied a career in writing if I couldn't get into veterinarian school. I had always planned to be a vet, but college was discouraged. Mom and Bob said the only reason a girl needed to go to college was to get her MRS degree. I knew I was going to be kicked out of the house when high school was over, but I had heard of student loans and community colleges so I kept hope that I might still get a college degree.

And of course I took a science course. I loved the labs with beakers, flasks, and microscopes, and the Bunsen burners were awesome too. It was heavenly, mixing up compounds and liquids and doing the experiments.

My Grandpa was the only one who shared my interest in chemistry. Actually, I don't know if he was really as interested in chemistry as he pretended to be. He was an enormous influence; truly, he was the best male role model I had growing up. He was a strong and decent man who raised three children during the Great Depression. He let me know he really loved me. He talked to me. He comforted me when my steer, Sonny Liston, was butchered and acknowledged my sorrow, but he explained that God put cattle on the earth for man's use and he made no apology for it.

I didn't get to see Grandpa very often as he and Grandma lived in Los Gatos, a couple of hours drive from us. But whenever I did see him, he always made time to talk to me.

Grandpa had a deep and resonating voice that could be scary, but he was as gentle as a mouse. When I was little I'd hide behind his recliner, and when I thought he was asleep I'd tickle the sparse gray hair on his nearly bald head. He always slapped himself and pretended it was a fly tickling him and that made me laugh.

He taught me things. He said no matter what I did, I should do it to the best of my ability. Even if I was just digging a ditch I should try to dig it with straight sides and a clean floor and to dig it better than anyone else.

Grandpa had endless patience. He got me started collecting coins. When he came to visit he would empty his pockets and we'd sit for hours going through each coin. Together we made several booklets of pennies, nickels, and dimes.

"You can tell the worth of a man by the condition of his tools," he used to say. "Some men will leave their tools outside in the weather where they'll rust and become useless. A good man will clean his tools and keep them neatly put away when he's not using them."

He was always good to Grandma. In fact, I never saw him upset or yell at anyone. He was patient and kind, he was good to me, and good with dogs.

"You can tell how a man will treat a woman by how he treats a dog," he said. "Find a man who is good to dogs."

And he told me I could be anything I set my mind to, and if I wanted to be a veterinarian, by God I would.

He held honesty above all else. "If a man's not honest," he said, "he's lost his soul."

"Always return things and you'll keep good neighbors," was another one.

Grandpa took me out to buy a dress for my sixth birthday. He picked it out. It was black velvet on top with a pink chiffon skirt. I'd never seen a dress like that, and I felt pretty wearing it. Grandpa was the only man who had ever told me I was beautiful.

I loved my Grandpa, and I knew he loved me.

Grandpa had a heart attack and died just after my fifteenth birthday. That may have been a blessing, really, because the last years of high school were terrible for me and I'm glad he didn't have to know what happened.

#

Bob continued to hit me when I least expected it. Once, because I was singing while I washed the dishes. Another time, he kicked me and sent me sprawling on the front lawn, because a neighborhood kid had stopped by for an unapproved visit, even though she had helped with my chores. I could never predict what would set him off. Staying out of trouble was like walking through a mine field.

Bob was working swing shift at Aerojet, which meant he left home at around 2:30 in the afternoon, and came home from work close to midnight. Night after night I had been having wild nightmares about space aliens and cats, vivid and long drawn-out nightmares. One night during a particularly violent dream, I woke up. I thought the dream had woken me, but then I heard Debbie whimpering. I sat up and as my eyes focused, I saw the figure of a man crouched by the side of her bed. Scared, I didn't say anything at first, but when the man didn't move I thought maybe it really wasn't a man. I called to Debbie and asked if she was all right. The figure stood up and hurried out of our room.

It was unmistakably Bob.

I asked Debbie again if she was okay, but she turned toward the wall and didn't answer me. I got out of bed and closed our door, then locked it, and went back to bed. I lay awake the rest of the night.

Debbie wouldn't tell me what had happened, but we entered into a silent agreement to lock our bedroom door every night. It wasn't a good security lock, and could easily be opened with a hairpin. Many nights Bob did open it, and I saw him in our room again and again. He was always at Debbie's bedside, sometimes just crouching, but sometimes he had his hands under the blankets. I discovered that when I moved or made enough noise to let him know I was awake he would leave, so I did that.

Weeks later Mom and Bob purchased a new king-sized bed for their room. They moved their old queen-sized bed into our pink bedroom, and the little twin beds were moved into Janie and Judy's bedroom. The little girls had finally outgrown their crib and youth beds and were excited to rearrange their room. I wasn't at all happy to share a bed with Debbie. Up until then Bob had never bothered me at night. Debbie wouldn't talk to me about what was going on when he came into our room, to her bed, but I knew it wasn't good. I told her to talk to Mom. She didn't. Then one night she and I were left home to babysit the little girls.

Judy went to sleep easily in her own twin bed, but Janie wouldn't stay in hers. It was common for Mom to take Janie into the master bedroom and lay down with her until she fell asleep, then carry her back to her own bed. Bob could not stand to have Janie cry under any circumstance, and bedtime was no exception. I was tired, so we agreed Debbie would lay down with Janie on Mom and Bob's bed until Janie went to sleep. Unfortunately, all four of us fell asleep like that. Me in my room, Judy in hers, Debbie and Janie in the master bedroom.

Bob came home before Mom and carried Janie into her own bed, then returned and got into bed with Debbie. Later, he told Mom he had thought it was her. He tried to convince Mom that he couldn't tell a sixteen-year-old girl's body from that of his wife, the mother of four children. They had a heck of an argument that night, but I stayed in my bed with the covers over my head.

Mom drove Debbie to our family doctor early the next morning to be examined, and when she returned Bob was spitting mad and yelling.

He screamed, "Why did you take her to *our* doctor? Now he knows you think I raped her."

Mom cried. Debbie cried. Bob's biggest concern was that our doctor knew what he had done. Mom had only been worried that Debbie might be pregnant. Debbie's feelings didn't seem to be of concern to either of them. She had been molested, and somehow they skipped right over the fact that she would be upset.

Now they'll get a divorce, I thought. But I was wrong.

Debbie got accused of being in love with Bob and enticing him, a story that was floated to our Grandma, who moved in with us shortly afterward to keep an eye on things.

For her part, Mom adopted a flat out denial of the fact that anything had occurred. She would cling to and nurture that denial for decades. Bob acted like he was the wounded party, the wrongfully accused.

I couldn't believe nothing was going to happen; no arrest, no divorce, nothing. I asked Mom what she was going to do about what had happened, what had been happening, and her response was, "It will be better for all of us, once you and Debbie are out of the house."

Oh, sure, I thought, *it's us stepping on your toes. And Debbie's being a real burden complaining about it, isn't she?*

Debbie wouldn't graduate high school for another year, two for me.

We kept locking our bedroom door, but there wasn't much else we could do to protect ourselves. We set up noise traps on the floor. I developed a profound and long-lasting insomnia. And Bob stayed out of our room.

Then one weekend morning I woke up and found I was alone in the house with Bob. I don't know where everyone else had gone, but I woke up in my room, alone in my queen-sized bed and I felt Bob get in and lay behind me. He reached over and pulled me into his groin. I could feel his erection on the back of my thighs. In a low hoarse voice he half-whispered, "I've always liked this bed the best."

I was terrified. I started hiccupping. Not normal little hiccups that come and go, these were big, deep ones that were almost like vomiting. If I'd had anything in my stomach I'm sure I would have thrown up. I tried to move away from his grip but he held me tight. I tried again, harder, and said, "I need to get some water." After a brief struggle, he let go of me. I went through the kitchen and wearing only my nightgown, I ran out to the barn and hid in the loft until Mom came home. I had been certain Bob would come after me, but he didn't.

Those high school years were unpleasant, except perhaps that I was developing a wicked sense of sarcasm and a bigger vocabulary.

Bob only hit or slapped me after that. He usually didn't leave marks, but when he blackened my eye a second time, my Journalism teacher asked me what had happened. I couldn't tell him so I looked at the floor. I wasn't trying to protect Bob, I was trying to protect myself. I was afraid if I told on Bob, he might kill me.

But Bob never sexually bothered me or Debbie again, as far as I know. We continued to lock our door every night and we were vigilant not to be alone with him in the house.

The day she graduated from high school, Debbie didn't just move away, she ran like the wind.

CHAPTER THIRTEEN

The Therapist

"How did that make you feel?"

"I felt like Mom should have called the police, or at least divorced him. She was obviously willing to throw Debbie and me away. I think she counted the days until we were out of the house. She wanted us gone so she could have her perfect little family," I explained.

"No," she smiled. "That's what you thought. I asked how it made you feel."

What? Oh, I see what you did there, that was tricky. Do all therapist ask how everything makes you feel?

"Okay, I was pissed off, and scared, is that what you're looking for?" I snapped.

"I can imagine," she answered, but still she just looked at me.

The room was quiet.

"Mostly scared." I clarified.

More silence.

"And helpless."

She still didn't speak.

Really? That's all you've got? No pearls of wisdom?

I was tired of talking about Bob the Step Monster.

"It *feels* like you think I should be having some big ah-ha moment, and it's not happening," I said, sure she was disappointed in my lack of insight.

The silence in the room was full of unspoken thoughts. Only the irritating ticking of the clock and the sound of my breathing.

"You were just a kid," she finally assessed. "There wasn't anything else you could do."

CHAPTER FOURTEEN

High School Graduation

My junior year of high school had been marked by fear and depression. I hadn't cared what I wore to school and I hardly washed my hair. No one spoke to me and I spoke to no one, which made for an amiable relationship. Eating lunch in the cafeteria was lonely, so I took to hiding out in the journalism room with my half sandwich. I was pathetic and I knew it.

I was less and less interested in classes, and I couldn't retain any of the information anyway. It wasn't like I didn't try. I'd read paragraph after paragraph, but at the end I couldn't remember any of the content. Tests were hopeless too; I would search the entire thing for even one question I could answer, and I made up stupid and sarcastic answers for the rest. I had always been good in school and couldn't figure out why it was so difficult for me now. I was exhausted all the time, sleepy during class, and I never did my homework.

My Government teacher that year was short and round with a big red face and jowls that trembled when he got mad, features that earned him the nickname Tomato Head. For reasons I never understood, he was mad at me pretty often. One day he was halfway through a tirade before I realized he was yelling at me. I hadn't done anything, so I was surprised to be the subject of his diatribe. I had been sitting quietly at my desk, not paying attention of course, but other than that I hadn't caused any trouble. And yet he was screaming at me. He said he wasn't going to put up with me anymore and had recommended to my counselor that I go to continuation school. Blah, blah, blah. He looked like he might explode, his face was so red. I'd been yelled at by a much scarier man than him. I felt nothing. Nothing at all, just–dull.

The last report card I got in June 1969 summarized my junior year grades. I had earned three F's, two D's, and one C.

The C was in Physical Education. It's pretty hard to screw up PE, unless you just don't go. It never occurred to me not to go, so as a happy consequence, I passed PE. I used to like the running and mostly the gymnastics, but all that year I just showed up. I decided I wasn't an average student after all, maybe I was stupid. Too stupid to pass high school anyway. Maybe I had only been a good student in the lower grades because the work was easy, and now I was seeing that I didn't really measure up. It was a depressing thought, but one I had to consider.

Debbie had moved in with our widowed grandmother, and I was very much alone. With no one to do all the inside work Debbie had been doing, new babysitters were hired who also did house chores. But I was still called upon to help out, most often with folding the laundry and putting it away. The first day I delivered Bob's socks to the top drawer of his dresser, I spotted a stack of envelopes that bore something familiar. Pushing his socks aside, I saw some were addressed to me and Debbie, and were from our father's parents. Other envelopes contained letters I had written to them, but had never been mailed. Anger mounted as I searched the opened cards sent from our grandparents, with references to checks they had contained and wishes to hear from us. The checks were all missing, and the letters were all dated in the early years of Mom and Bob's marriage, stopping a couple of years afterward.

"What are you doing?" Mom asked. She had just come into her room.

"What are these?" I held out the stack of letters accusingly.

She sighed. "You shouldn't be snooping in Bob's dresser."

"Why has he got cards and letters with my name on them?" I countered. "These are all opened, and the checks have been taken. I've never even seen these letters. What is HE doing with them?"

"That was my decision," she stated. "I thought since you and Debbie wanted to take Bob's name, we should make the change complete, so no one would know you were step children."

"YOUR decision? You decided they didn't need to get the letters I wrote to them? Anyone who looks at this family can tell Debbie and I are step-kids, just by the way you treat us, and besides, it wasn't our idea to change our names. How could you make a decision like that?"

I was livid. But it didn't matter, without another word, she turned and left the room. I took the stack of letters and hid them in my closet.

#

All that previous year Mom and Bob had threatened to sell Red if I didn't bring my grades up, and by the time Debbie left, it had become less of a threat and more a certainty.

I didn't want to, but I knew I was going to have to sell Red myself. I couldn't let Mom and Bob have the satisfaction; they would enjoy the opportunity and would have likely kept that money too.

I had a dentist appointment right after I'd made that decision. I thought I'd better ask every adult I knew if they might want to buy Red, and the dentist was the first person I saw. It wasn't that my dentist was a horseman, or even my first or best choice to own Red. None of that factored in to why I asked him. I didn't really even think he'd be interested. He just happened to be the first person I came across after I'd made my decision.

He surprised me when he said he would like to buy a horse for his daughter who was a couple of years younger than me. He asked how much I wanted for Red and I said $200. I thought I could have gotten more but I wanted to be sure *I* was the one to sell him, so I set the price low. The dentist surprised me again when he said he wanted to come out and see Red over the weekend.

He arrived alone in a truck, pulling a nice horse trailer. I showed him how gentle Red was and rode him around without a saddle or bridle, all the time with a big lump in my throat. When I slid off Red's back, the dentist said we had a deal.

I fought back tears as I loaded Red into the trailer and all my muscles were tense and aching and I was suddenly so tired I could barely raise my arms or move my legs. Red hesitated when his front feet were on the trailer ramp and without thinking I slapped his rump. My breath caught in my throat. I had never hit Red before in any manner, and even though he probably didn't even notice it through all his muscle and hair I was mad at myself for slapping him now; the last time I would ever see him. Then Red walked into the trailer by himself, like he wanted to go.

I went into the trailer with Red and whispered to him how sorry I was and that I'd miss him. I stroked his neck and back, felt his soft nose one last time. I tried to hide the tears I now couldn't stop. It wasn't Red's fault. It wasn't Red's fault I couldn't keep him at my house. It wasn't Red's fault I couldn't keep him forever. I told him I was sorry, so, so sorry. My heart burst and I buried my face in the warm hair on his hip, and cried like I'd never cried before. I always refused to cry when Bob hit me, but this hurt was different and for some reason I couldn't stop.

It took several minutes before I could collect myself. When I came out of the trailer the dentist asked if I had changed my mind and I shook my head no. He said I could come visit Red any time I liked and I knew I never would. I looked at a cloud in the distance and wished that he would just please drive off and leave me before I lost control again.

Then, seeming to read my thoughts, he did drive off. I watched the dust swirl behind the trailer as it went down the road and out of sight, just as I had watched Gene's empty trailer disappear three years before. I walked back into Red's barn and was struck by his lingering scent and the chunks of his hair caught in the boards of the stall and his feed bucket and the horse dung and it was all too much. I fell in a heap on his leftover hay and cried myself out. I wished my Grandpa had been alive to help me. He would have known what to say, he alone could have comforted me.

As usual, when I got home nobody mentioned Red. They figured it out a couple of days later when they noticed I hadn't gone to feed him. Later that summer Mom and Bob bought

Judy a sweet little dapple grey pony named Dolly. Then they bought Janie a larger roan pony named Strawberry. There was never a doubt both Dolly and Strawberry would live in the pasture at The Property. I didn't bother asking them about the obvious inequity; by then I knew there were different rules for Debbie and me. I wanted to be upset that I had to feed those ponies, while Janie and Judy stayed in bed in the mornings, but I couldn't be mad. It wasn't their fault they had been born holding a lucky ticket. I knew they had an idyllic childhood with two parents who loved them, unlike Debbie or me.

I had watched Mom pay bills once while I was helping out with the inside chores, and found out that the mortgage on the house and property was $86 a month. I was good enough with money to realize they were still getting $75 from my father in child support until I graduated, and that was the only reason I was still there at all. They were making out like fat rats off that child support.

The next fall I began my senior and last year of high school. It was still early in the morning on the first day when I was called out of class to go to my counselor's office. I hated being called out over the loud speaker, and not because I was afraid I'd miss something important in class. I figured it was probably Bob demanding another skirt check or some other kind of problem and it was all so incredibly embarrassing. I walked as slowly as I could down the empty corridors, then was ushered into the familiar administration office, then even further into the bowels of the main building and into the cramped office cluttered with books that belonged to my counselor. He asked how I was doing and I said fine, like I always said. I slumped in the chair opposite him.

"I understand you sold your horse." It wasn't a question, it was a statement. I didn't have to wonder how he knew. I was sure Bob had told him, bragged probably.

"Yeah," I responded.

I studied the floor tiles; they were those square linoleum ones and had worn unevenly, particularly where the chair legs moved back and forth.

"I've been looking through your transcripts," he continued. He had opened a folder on his desk, and pointed to something.

I knew he wanted me to stand up and look at the folder, but I didn't see the need for that; I knew what was in there—I was failing—I hadn't given my report card to my Mom without looking at it first, and I'd been punished for exactly what it revealed. I was waiting for him to tell me I'd have to finish high school at the continuation school for bad kids and idiots, just like Tomato Head had recommended.

"I've done some checking, and you have almost all the credits you need to graduate," he said. "You've got all the required classes and enough credits with your electives, the only thing you need to graduate is one semester of Physical Education," he paused. I could sense him looking at me, but I chose to continue studying the tiles. "I tried to get that waived, but the state requires all the PE credits." He paused again. I stayed silent, trying to process what he had just said.

"Kathi, what I'm saying is I want you to graduate. I want you to get your diploma."

This sounded a lot like the beginning of a lecture, and I'd already been lectured on my grades. I couldn't think of anything he might say that would instantly make me smarter. However, I did notice that one of the floor tiles had broken and dirt and grime had filled in the empty space. I also noticed how the other three corners were beat up and ragged because this one was broken. For some reason, I thought about my sisters.

"Kathi, I want to get you out of here. I want to get you out of here in the shortest time possible, or I'm afraid you won't graduate at all."

I vaguely thought he wanted me out of his office, and my first thought was I should get up and leave. But he hadn't actually said I should leave and his voice didn't sound mad, so I wasn't sure what I was supposed to do.

"If you can agree to come to school for one hour a day this fall semester you can graduate in January and get out of here. Can you do that? Can you come to school for one hour a day?" he asked. "I can get it scheduled as your first class in the morning, if that will help."

I didn't look up, but my brain was buzzing. Was this good news or bad news? Bob probably wouldn't let me stay at home just to go to school one hour a day. Worse, where would I go when I graduated in January? I didn't have a car yet, and I just...I didn't know how I could possibly do it. But I *was* failing all my classes, and Tomato Head *was* threatening to send me away, which didn't sound good except maybe I could live at the continuation school, which might not be so bad, or maybe it would. And if I did only go to school for one hour a day, it meant I'd be home the rest of the day and that wasn't good either, because Bob would be home during the day.

It was too much to think about. I went back to studying the floor.

The counselor apparently hadn't planned for me to make a decision.

"I know the conditions your step-father has made, that you have to move out, and I've arranged for you to live with one of our English teachers, at least in the short term. She has agreed you can stay with her until you finish this semester and graduate. I'll take you out there now, she's expecting you." He stood up and I followed him out. I had no idea where I was going, but I'd learned long ago not to think. I just did what I was told.

He drove me home to get my things. When he parked in front of the house I could see a cardboard box about the size of an orange crate on the porch steps in front of the door.

When I opened the box I saw it contained some of my clothes. No personal items, none of the letters from my grandparents, or my horse books, not even the Indian beads I'd collected, just two pairs of jeans and a few old t-shirts, some socks and panties. I was already wearing my only pair of shoes. And my Karo syrup jar. It was clear that someone already knew about this arrangement and hadn't bothered to tell me. I was hurt, but I was more surprised they had given me my money. I tested the door knob, and found it was locked, even though I knew Bob was home.

That was the fall of 1969. I was sixteen years old, and like trash, I'd been thrown out of my home. Like the trash I'd been dumping every week, even my papers had been sorted and burned. I was stunned only in how fast it had happened. I'd known about this for the past ten years. That verbal contract—just a statement really—was iron-clad with no negotiating the terms. In the blink of an eye, I was out of the house.

I did my one hour a day at school in the mornings, as my counselor had promised. I was safe and comfortable. Colors seemed dull, and nothing much interested me. I marked off the days like an institutionalized prisoner worried about being released on parole. There was so much I didn't know. I didn't know how to buy food, or cook, so I ate what Terry offered and didn't complain. I tried to be helpful. I was quiet. And I slept. I found I could sleep for hours on end.

There were many days when I stared at the street full of passing cars and wondered if I would ever figure out what so many other people obviously managed without too much effort. I needed to buy a car. But to get a car you need money, and to get money, you need a job, and to get a job—and here was my problem—you need a car. I didn't see how to get from point A to point C. I knew it was obviously an attainable objective, because so many people were able to manage it, but for the life of me I couldn't see a way out of this endless loop.

The summer before I left The Property, Bob had purchased two old retired Forestry Vans—1959 International Travel-All Trucks—at an auction for $300 each. One was in pretty good shape and he sold it to our neighbor for $600. The other truck had a blown transmission and would only drive in reverse. Mom suggested I try to buy it and as much as I didn't want to ask Bob for anything at all, I finally did. After delaying his answer for a period of time that was designed to irritate a prospective buyer, Bob, having no other offers, agreed to sell it to me for what he paid for it, $300. I had that much money left in my Karo syrup jar and I paid it without haggling. Grandma agreed to loan me the money to fix the transmission. I drove that clunker—in reverse—all the way to Scotty's Transmission in downtown Orangevale where they got it running forward again for $290.

Living with Terry worked well until I graduated in the middle of January 1970. I was seventeen years old, and completely out of high school, and I knew I needed to find my own place.

I had been angry with Mom for a long time, but I had always hoped that she disagreed with the way Bob treated us. Even if that were the case, clearly, she hadn't been able to bring herself to do anything about it. My best guess is she remembered being poor, when Debbie and I were little, and I supposed she didn't want to go back to struggling like that with four kids to raise. Bob represented a financial security she could not, would not, turn away from no matter how bad things had gotten. Besides, from her point of view, we had survived. Bob would never hurt his own daughters, and Debbie and I were now safely out of the house. So Mom thought it would all be smooth sailing now, and she seemed willing to do what she could to help us, as long as that help didn't require money.

CHAPTER FIFTEEN

The Therapist

"That was a pivotal year for you. Selling your horse, leaving home. How did that make you feel?"

I was sure my expression was answer enough. I barely avoided rolling my eyes.

"Yes. Well. How did that make me feel? I don't think I felt much during those days," I answered.

She looked at me. I tried to read her mind but failing that, I just sat and looked back at her.

"That's not true. You must know, not everyone would have reacted the way you did. You took control of the sale of your horse. That had to have been very difficult to do."

"I didn't want them to win. It was the only option I could think of at the time," I answered.

She was quiet for a moment while she studied me.

"You're very resilient. You should be proud of that," she finally said.

For some reason, my throat tightened. I had no words. I looked back at the covered window.

CHAPTER SIXTEEN

Money

Debbie wanted to come back from our grandmother's home, and Mom located a duplex in Rocklin that was for rent. It was conveniently located across the street from Sierra Community College and cost only seventy-five dollars a month. The price was right, and with our dwindling savings, Debbie and I signed the lease and enrolled in a couple of classes for that spring semester. Things looked good, with one minor issue. We had no jobs.

We were on our own for the first time in our lives, and being seventeen and eighteen year olds, we did all the predictable things. We drank. We smoked pot (which was plentiful). And we met boys. I wasn't promiscuous by any means, and remained shy, but I found one willing participant who ironed out any remaining questions I had about sex. To my relief, I discovered that not all men have flaccid, diseased penises in their pants.

Our pressing money problem was made slightly worse by Debbie's purchase of a car. She paid $250 for an old Ford something-or-other which to my knowledge, never went anywhere. She finally gave up, and abandoned it on the roadside.

We still had my car, and hitchhiking was an acceptable method of transportation back then, so we managed to get by with just one vehicle for some time.

But to pay the rent we needed cash and one night we decided to pull up our socks and drive to San Francisco, act like drug lords, and make a bundle of money all in one go. We pooled our money and decided that between us we had $250 to risk. We were told by someone we thought must know, that for that much money we could buy a kilo of pot, which could then be split into "two finger baggies" and the entire proceeds should net us double our money.

Neither of us had a clue how big a kilo was, so we took the back seat out of the Travel-All, thinking it might be the size of a bale of hay, and set off. We arrived in the city limits of San Francisco about an hour and a half later at around midnight, high as kites, and looking to score. The place was amazing. Crazy people danced in the streets, hippies smoked pot openly. Music played everywhere. It felt like being in a movie. Or a fairground. Except for the traffic, it hardly looked like a city. We laughed like mad at everything, and asked anyone with long hair where we could make a buy—lingo we'd picked up from our friend who knew such things. Somehow we found a guy who knew another guy and we got our kilo, which was considerably smaller than a bale of hay, and we drove home. As we drove, the pot wore off and paranoia set in. Do you think we got ripped off? What if we get busted? Oh my God! We just passed a cop!

Near home, we stopped and picked up a box of zip lock sandwich baggies and a couple of cute hitchhikers.

The hitchhikers turned out to be quite useful, as they knew how to separate the pot and take out the seeds and stems, and how much to put into each baggie. We put them to work, and by the wee early morning hours we had pot on every counter of the kitchen, all over the table, on the floor, and we had eaten everything in the refrigerator and cupboards except a can of Crisco. We had bags of pot ready to sell to make our fortune. We made spaghetti and put the pot dust into the sauce and, after giving the hitchhikers some joints for the road, we deposited them back onto the interstate to continue their journey. After a quick trip through the Jack-in-the-Box drive through, we returned home and tried to clean the place up. Unfortunately, we were stoned again and tired. All we managed was a face-plant onto our Jumbo Jacks and fries. We woke up hours later, hearing a knock on the door. It was Grandma.

Ho-ly Shit. Debbie grabbed the baggies of pot and hid them in the bedroom and began straightening up while I answered the door and tried to act casual. Grandma came in and greeted us with her usual hugs and kisses, and I swept pot off the kitchen chair so she could sit down. Debbie bolted toward the bathroom.

"What are you girls cooking?" she asked eyeing the saucepan on the stove. My heart stopped.

"Spaghetti," I said, trying to sound nonchalant. I took off the lid and stirred. Then I had a moment of conscience. I had just borrowed money from Grandma to fix my truck, and it would be rude not to offer her some lunch. I thought it was safe enough, and certainly she would decline.

"Would you like some?" I asked.

"Sure," she said happily.

Oh God, I thought, and my heart froze for the second time. When it restarted it was slamming fast and hard in my chest and I was sure Grandma could hear it. Everywhere I looked there was pot dust, flakes, and seeds. I kept stirring the sauce.

"Okay."

I couldn't think of a way out, so I scooped up three plates of spaghetti and placed them on the table. When Debbie came back into the kitchen, her face was pale, and she looked sick. She asked what we were doing.

"Eating lunch," I offered and nodded for her to sit down at the table. I forced a smile at Debbie.

Grandma ate every bite on her plate, then after a quick chat she kissed us good bye and drove off. Later we asked her what she had done that afternoon, and she said she couldn't remember, then she asked what we had done.

"Cleaned house," we replied.

We sold the pot and paid the rent, but our landlord who lived in the duplex next door said we had made noise all night, had strange men in the house, and he didn't want hippies living next to his family. Though we were excited to be called hippies, we couldn't deny any of his more damning accusations. We were evicted.

We found a shack in Folsom, a small town that borders Orangevale, that rented for sixty dollars a month. It was in the middle of town, which was better for getting jobs, but continuing my classes at the college was going to be a secondary issue. But, first things first, I needed an income.

I applied for and got a job working for the Orangevale veterinarian, the one I had always used when Red needed shots, or a cut stitched up. I was hired to clean dog poop from the kennels and empty the trash, both were tasks I was well trained for. The job only required a few hours a day and paid about twenty-five dollars a week, not a lot of money, but enough, and it left time for me to go to school.

I thought I'd gotten the job on my own, but Mom later bragged that she had talked the vet into hiring me. So apparently, on my own, I wasn't even capable of being hired to pick up dog shit. Splendid. Learning that was so good for my ego.

With my rent only thirty dollars a month, I was able to pay Grandma back in just a couple of months and I was proud of that. And I completed one of the two classes I was taking at Sierra College. I had enrolled in Animal Husbandry and I put a lot of effort into my papers, which resulted in a B for that class. I was really excited because it made me realize I wasn't completely stupid after all. Unfortunately, I had to drop the other class, Field Crops Management, because the class conflicted with my work hours.

The job with the veterinarian lasted until the middle of summer. I borrowed twenty-eight cents from a dish on the secretary's desk to get a gallon of gas, because my truck had been on empty for a day and a half. They were nice people, and if they had been there I would have asked for the change, and I think they would have let me borrow it or maybe even given it to me as an advance, but it was after hours and I couldn't get home any other way. They fired me. I was mortified. I had planned to tell them the next day, and even as they fired me I promised to pay it back, but they had already decided to let me go and handed me my final check. Grandpa would have been so ashamed of me. Devastated and embarrassed, I was unemployed again.

Once more, Mom intervened.

CHAPTER SEVENTEEN

Brian

Debbie moved to Kentucky with a friend, a change that left me on my own and more uncertain of my future than ever. Mom came by a few weeks later and said a man she worked with could help me find a job and she offered to drive me to meet him. She failed to mention he was located over a hundred miles away. When we drove into the Santa Rosa Fairgrounds, her friend, a short-statured man named Juan, came up to the car accompanied by a tall kid in a black cowboy hat. They seemed quite pleased to see the two of us. Mom and her friend went one direction and this kid, Brian, and I went another. I still don't know where Mom went, as I didn't see her again for months. Within a few hours it became obvious I'd been abandoned again, at a fairground of all places. That was evidently where my mom had decided I should work.

Brian was a big talker, quite attractive, and I was comfortable enough in his presence. I was slightly concerned when he borrowed money from someone to buy me lunch, but hey, that was his choice and I was hungry and broke. Brian walked me through the process of getting a groomers license so I could work with the race horses, and I got a job working in the horse barns that very afternoon. Brian was nice enough, and he looked out for me like it was his job. Two weeks later I hitch-hiked home to get my truck and moved out of the shack in Folsom.

Brian and I continued to travel the race horse circuit, moving from Santa Rosa to Bay Meadows, then Cal Expo, and after knowing him for only three months, he proposed to me. Marriage had never been on my personal To Do list, but it was clear I hadn't been doing a very good job of taking care of myself and I showed only minimal signs of improvement.

I could be a reliable employee, but hadn't proved to be capable of doing anything that required a brain. I had done well in the only college class I completed, but I didn't have enough money to continue. I could pay bills and keep a balance sheet, but I still didn't have a bank account or know how to write a check. Brian was nice, he made sure I ate every day, didn't hit or yell at me, and he was nice to dogs. I really didn't see the benefit of going under contract, but I worried if I refused, how I would survive. He made sure I had food, water, shelter, and most importantly, friendship.

Marrying Brian looked like the best and only option I had.

I said yes.

Brian was the middle son of three boys born to an upper middle class family in Central Sacramento. Their home was beautiful, expensively decorated, but no one else in Brian's family was a cowboy; a fact I found mildly confusing. His father Kenny, a very quiet, dignified man who was a career army guy, had retired as a Major. His mother, Margurite, was a well-kept woman who looked to me like she had never worked a day in her life. She was a fussy Doris Day type homemaker, except she smoked like a chimney. She served up coffee in real teacups with saucers and always wore a dress with an apron tied around her waist. Margurite told me she was a bit distressed she'd only had sons to raise, and said she would have really enjoyed having a daughter. But as she looked me over, I was certain I wasn't what she had hoped for.

Brian was only nineteen years old when we announced to his parents that we wanted to get married, and in California boys had to be a minimum of 21 to marry without having parental permission. Oddly, girls only needed to be sixteen. Because of this, his parents decided they needed to meet my parents and discuss the problem amongst themselves. His parents set a date with Mom and Bob, then we loaded up and drove to The Property in Orangevale. It was a most bizarre meeting.

Right off the bat, Kenny asked why I wasn't still living at home. I moved to the edge of my seat waiting to hear how Mom and Bob would answer. Mom sat mute. Bob eventually sputtered fragmented sentences about having a full house with two children of his own…graduated high school…money issues…no more child support, then just trailed off.

There it was.

I felt vindicated somehow that he had finally confirmed out loud that I had only been a paycheck and had never really been considered a member of his family.

Then Bob suggested in a much more declarative voice, "She could always join the army." He seemed quite pleased with this idea.

The Army? Seriously? I was shocked. We were eyeball deep in Vietnam and he was suggesting I join the Army? I hated guns and the only thing I knew with any certainty about Vietnam were stories of boys my age disappearing to Canada to *evade* the draft. But then I thought, *of course, he'd be happy to ship me off to Vietnam.*

"Lots of boys my age joined the service when we were right out of high school, myself included. It gave us structure and kept us out of trouble and...." Bob went on happily.

"Excuse me," Kenny cut him off and stared directly at him, "Unless things have changed since I retired, *from the Army*, the service won't accept her until she's eighteen."

"Oh, well, she'll be eighteen in just a couple of months," Bob was quick to point out.

A cease fire followed while the adults gave each other the stink eye.

Finally, Kenny countered, "I don't know Kathi very well but I don't think that's a viable option." He continued, "Are you really suggesting she join the Army?"

More silence.

"Bob, you served during peacetime," Kenny's voice, usually quiet, had taken on a commanding tone. He crossed his arms and leaned back in his chair.

Bob nodded yes, but didn't speak.

"And what type of duty were you assigned?" Kenny inquired.

Bob hung his head and picked at some non-existent speck on the table. "Clerical." He shrugged his shoulders and twisted his mouth.

Kenny turned toward me, peered over his glasses, and demanded, "Do you *want* to join the Army?"

It felt like a courtroom. Nobody ever asked my opinion about anything. I could honestly say I had never even thought about joining the Army. In particular, I had never imagined being a bullet dodger in the jungle. "No," I answered. I hoped I sounded decisive.

I was suddenly scared that being a minor, Bob could enlist me without my consent, and I pictured myself in camouflage gear with a giant backpack and a gun, and twigs sprouting from my helmet.

But Kenny's hands slapped the table with the authority of a drill sergeant as he declared, "That's it then. We don't have anything else to discuss."

He and Margurite got up and left. The next day they signed the marriage application, and Brian and I were married a couple of weeks later, a couple of weeks before my eighteenth birthday.

Brian seemed angry and confrontational with his mother most of the time. I wondered if all kids were angry with their parents. Even though I was slightly intimidated by Kenny, he and Margurite seemed like really good parents. They were pleasant to each other and spoke kindly to their three sons. They didn't live on a farm so I didn't understand how Brian had turned into a cowboy. I finally determined he was on some sort of rebellious kick and was trying out this western identity, and I wondered how long it would last.

When I asked Margurite about Brian's history, she told me he had done very well in high school and had been on track to pursue an engineering degree his wealthy godfather was anxious to fund. She showed me pictures and he certainly looked like a normal, clean cut boy when he graduated high school. But sometime afterward, Brian had rejected the idea of college to become a cowboy.

His passion was to be a very old cowboy. He had developed a convincing southern drawl, wore all the appropriate cowboy gear, had a penchant for guns and expensive rodeo equipment, didn't mind missing a few showers and shaves, and somewhere along the line, he had managed to acquire a good working knowledge of horses. He was very good with them. I never discovered how he had achieved the transformation and naively believed it would end at some point. But it never did. In fact, he became even more entrenched, occasionally making up stories about things that never happened including names of people he had never met. I thought his behavior was a little odd, but he wasn't hurting anyone, so I thought, *if the boy wants to be a cowboy what's the harm.*

One day Margurite pulled me aside and said she was concerned about Brian. She confided that she believed he had psychological problems, and probably should see a psychiatrist.

"What kind of problems?" I was sure she was about to explain his unusual lifestyle.

"He has issues with saying good-bye," she claimed.

Hmm, I'm going to need a little more information.

"You think he can't say good-bye?" I queried.

"No, he can say it. But whenever someone gets ready to leave, he hides under his bed."

I laughed out loud. Margurite folded her arms and waited for me to stop.

"Well, surely that was when he was a little kid, Margurite, I've seen his bed and I don't think he could get under it now," I continued laughing at the image.

She lit up a cigarette and looked ready to punch me in the mouth.

"I left him to get my truck a few weeks ago, and I can't swear to it but I didn't see him get under the bed," I offered. I knew I was mocking her, but I couldn't help it. "I suppose he could have been under there the whole time I was gone, but he was upright when I got back."

She turned on her heel, poured herself a cup of coffee and the conversation ended. It was certainly true Brian exhibited behavior I couldn't explain, and as time went by I wished I had taken Margurite's concerns seriously and allowed her to discuss them in more depth. Unfortunately, that was all she ever said on the subject.

#

Brian and I drove to Santa Cruz one Saturday. I had explained to him about losing contact with my grandparents on my father's side, and he suggested we look them up. The last time I'd been to their home I was either six or seven years old and it was a long shot that I'd even find their place—a duplex near the ocean with an avocado tree in the back yard—but I was eager to try. They lived on a side street near the Boardwalk, and sure enough, we found it. I felt nervous as we rang the doorbell.

They had no idea who I was. Even after I told them, there was no warmth. I introduced Brian and they shook his hand.

"Well, what is it you want?" my Grandfather asked me.

"Nothing. I, it's just been...I never cashed those checks you sent...I, um, I didn't..." I hadn't rehearsed what to say, and with my social retardation, I had trouble finding the words.

After what seemed like a breath of a second, Grandpa thanked us for stopping by and hustled us out the door, my grandmother never even left her seat.

The visit had been a colossal failure. Too much time had passed. The hurt must have run extraordinarily deep. I wanted to explain that I never got their letters, but I had blown my only chance. I'm sure they thought I wanted money. When we got home, I wrote them a letter, explaining what had happened, and asking if we could please stay in touch. I thought if they read it, they would understand. I'd always been able to write better than I could speak. But they never wrote back.

Seven months after we married, I discovered I was pregnant.

Brian and I lived just a step above homelessness; we had lived in tack rooms on the track, and when moving from one track to another we had slept in the back of the boss' truck.

But with a baby on the way, we needed something more respectable. Brian found a job on a thoroughbred horse breeding farm in southern Sacramento, which bordered the Delta River. It had a tiny, furnished efficiency apartment at the far end of the farm, and even though it was only 300 square feet of living space, the indoor plumbing represented a big uptick in living style for us. I had little to do those days except percolate a baby and feed the ranch dogs.

I admit I enjoyed being on the farm all day with the horses and trees and pastures. It was all very serene and easy. It gave me time to think about the fact I was only nineteen years old and question what I wanted for myself and my baby's future, and the one thing I kept coming back to was school. I had been an excellent student in grade school and junior high, and it was only when I reached high school that I'd stumbled badly, and I spent a good deal of time trying to understand why. It made me mad to think how brain dead I had been back then. I was sure if I could re-take those classes now, I could do better.

Whatever the case, I wouldn't have the chance to do anything about school until after the baby was born. Even then, it seemed a distant desire. I decided I definitely wanted to get a college degree, but I didn't have any particular field of interest other than wanting to be a veterinarian. I had other interests too, in case I couldn't be a vet. I liked numbers; maybe I could work in a bank. I liked writing stories too. Or maybe I could be a stand-up comic, except I had stage fright. What I realized was, I wasn't very good at figuring out what I wanted, and that was really getting in the way of me setting a goal.

#

When I was six months pregnant, Brian and I got arrested. Unbeknownst to me, we had driven to the home of a gun seller. Brian purchased a handgun while I stayed in the car. I wasn't aware that he was buying a gun, and was quite surprised when he slid into the driver's seat and proudly waved it in my face. When I asked why he needed a gun, he had no reason except that he made the money so it was his to spend and he liked guns. It was a big, silver automatic piece and I was shocked. If he had presented me with a dead cat I wouldn't have been more surprised. We were in Brian's old 1957 Chevy sedan, which had a bench seat, and I scooted as far to the opposite side as I could, then considered getting out of the car.

"It's not gonna hurt you," he said disgustedly. "See? It's not even loaded."

He did something and the thing that held the bullets fell out of the gun's handle. Then he pulled the top back like I had seen in the movies. I knew exactly zero about guns, and wasn't convinced it still couldn't fire. I stayed where I was.

"What are you going to do with it? You can't carry it in the car," I wanted him to sell it back to whoever he'd bought it from.

"It'll be fine," he said. "The law states it can't be loaded or *concealed* in a motor vehicle, but it's legal to transport a gun, how else can you get them from one place to another?"

His statement seemed reasonable. Brian put the empty bullet holder back into the gun and laid the thing on the seat between us, and we set off for home. It was dusk, and traffic was heavy. I couldn't stand to look at it so I distracted myself by staring out the side window at the passing farm fields.

We had just gotten on the freeway when suddenly, the car filled with red and blue light from behind and a loud siren blasted close behind our car. Startled, Brian swerved. It was a cop. Brian didn't pull over right away, even though we were traveling in the far right lane, instead, he slowed and began madly fidgeting with the gun with his right hand, which caused the car to drift back and forth as we proceeded down the freeway. He finally got the bullet holder out of the gun, leaned across me, and threw it into the glove box. Then he laid the rest of the gun back on the seat between us and pulled onto the shoulder of the road.

The officer came up to Brian's window, shined his flashlight into the car and went into high holy freaking cop mode. He drew his gun. He called for backup. He screamed at us. Brian had his hands in the air and was trying to tell the young cop that he'd just bought the gun, a detail I didn't think was particularly helpful, given the circumstances.

THE OLIVE PICKER · 115

Within minutes our car was surrounded, we were roughly dragged onto the side of the road, handcuffed, and hauled off to the Sacramento City Jail. After processing, I was allowed a phone call.

Mom had told Debbie and me many, many, times that if we ever got into trouble with the police not to bother calling her. So I called Margurite. She answered the phone in her usual cheerful voice and asked what we kids were up to. Poor thing, she dropped and broke one of her expensive dinner plates when I told her we were locked up in the county jail.

We were released later that night on our own recognizance. Kenny obtained a lawyer for us in the morning, and the charges were eventually dropped after a thorough explanation and confirmation of the facts. Brian bragged about the experience to anyone who would listen; then he obtained a concealed weapons permit so he would avoid having that problem again in the future. I was absolutely certain never buying another gun again was a more effective preventive strategy than the permit, and why in the hell did anyone but a bank robber need a gun like that anyway?

My arguments were a total waste of words. Brian defended his gun purchase as being his hobby, and he couldn't *believe* I would suggest he deny himself the pursuit of *his* hobby.

I knew then that I really shouldn't be married to this cowboy-gangster, but once again I had nowhere else to go and with a baby on the way, my choices were limited.

Kenny died of a heart attack only a month later. I was sad about that, as he had been a very decent man and had treated me quite fair.

With the money Brian received from Kenny's will a couple of months later, we purchased a single wide mobile home and moved to a trailer park. In my wildest dreams, I had never expected to ever live in a mobile home. I was nine months pregnant, unemployed, and living in a trailer park with a bunch of guns and a cowboy. We had no phone, and only one vehicle, an old truck that Brian had traded for his car to better suit his needs.

My due date was February 1st, 1973, and I had a doctor's appointment that day. That morning my feet were so swollen I couldn't wear shoes so I crammed my chubby toes into a pair of wooly slipper socks and waited for Brian to come pick me up. The doctor weighed me, told me I'd gained too much weight just like he did at every other appointment, and gave me some pills to relieve the water retention. I hobbled back out to the truck and we drove home.

I walked into our mobile home at 2:50 in the afternoon. It was exactly 3:00 o'clock when I popped the pills the doctor had given me, then took off my slipper socks. Brian had driven the truck back to work. Before I got down the hall, I peed all over myself in a great gush.

Wow, I thought, *those pills work fast*.

Within seconds, a pain rippled across my lower back and stomach, and then it was gone. Had my water just broken? I had read about labor and water breaking but the funny thing was, I never *really* expected it to happen. I realized I didn't have a plan. As another pain rippled across my lower back, I decided I needed to come up with one pretty quick.

Brian was gone, and wouldn't be back near a phone for at least 30 minutes, which meant he would be no help. I looked out the window, and only saw one home that showed signs of life—the one across the street where a woman ran a day care for about twenty kids. I waddled over and asked to use her phone to call my doctor, who told me to go immediately to the hospital. Hanging up, I knew my neighbor had listened to my conversation and I hoped she would give me some advice, but the tired old thing was doing her very best to fake attention toward the children as she hustled me out the door and said goodbye. I was on my own.

I walked down the middle of the street barefooted, looking for another mobile home with an occupant, anyone who might have a car. Suddenly a monster pain roared across my back and abdomen nearly taking me to my knees. Apparently, I needed to think of a faster plan. Beyond the trailer park a fairly busy freeway bordered the front gate. That was the closest I was to other people and moving cars.

I made my way to the road and stuck out my thumb. I was a ridiculous cliché. *Why hadn't I made a plan?* I didn't even have my purse with me, I'd left it at home when I'd gone to make the phone call. Why didn't I have *shoes*? I had nothing with me, I was barefoot and hideously pregnant. I hoped a police car or a taxi would drive by. Neither did. The next car approaching was a red sports car. Thankfully, the driver slowed, and pulled to the side of the road beside me. It was a bright red Corvette. The driver powered down the passenger window, leaned over, and with his eyes bulging from their sockets, asked, "Are you pregnant?"

Duh. I thought of a sarcastic answer and was about to smart off when another pain doubled me over on the side of the road, as I clutched my stomach.

"Do you need to get to the hospital?" he asked helplessly. He seemed nice but dim-witted. He sprinted around the front of his car and bent down to speak to me. Dazed from the pain, I was acutely aware of the resonance of the car's throaty exhaust system and leaned my head against the fender. The vibration was rather comforting.

"Yes," I squeezed out through gritted teeth, as I struggled to stand.

He opened the passenger door and it occurred to me that I'd never ridden in a Corvette before. I contemplated how exactly I might lower my bulky load down into a seat that was only two inches off the ground. I realized I was in no position to be fussy about the suitability of the ride, and more importantly, grace definitely could not be a consideration. With the guy holding my arm, I flopped in like a dead fish, just as another pain hit. I may have left claw marks on his dash.

"Where's the hospital?" He asked as he revved the engine and dropped it into gear.

Another contraction gripped me, and I was paralyzed with pain. *So sorry,* I thought, *can't chat right now.*

"Please, lady, just tell me which direction to go," he begged.

I wished I could tell him, but I wasn't sure. I had never driven there. I'd been the airhead who just rode in the passenger seat and enjoyed the scenery. *Seriously,* I told myself, *you've got to start paying more attention.*

Even though the weather was cool, my hair was becoming wet with sweat. With herculean effort, I raised my head marginally, and through squinted eyes I looked at the road ahead. I wiggled my right index finger in the universal 'straight ahead' signal.

"This way?" he asked.

I nodded. The pain was excruciating and constant now.

The engine roared and as the car leapt forward, and the thrust mashed me instantly against the seat. My eyes widened with pain as I screamed out.

"I'm sorry, I'm sorry, I just want to get you there fast." He seemed to have gathered himself together a bit. "Have you been timing your pains?"

Well, that would seem a reasonable thing to do if A.) I had a watch, and B.) If they weren't coming one on top of another. I shook my head, no.

We ripped down the freeway at warp speed and from the corner of my eye, I recognized the turn just as we passed it. "There," I squeaked.

The guy spun the car 180 degrees right in the middle of the freeway, I don't think he even looked for oncoming traffic. Down the side road he could see a hospital sign and asked "St. John's Hospital? Is that it?"

I was out of my head; the pain was unrelenting. I didn't care if it was the right hospital or even a veterinary hospital. Right now it was the right hospital. I nodded and we flew into the emergency bay on what seemed like two wheels. When he opened my door the dust was still flying around the car. I had all the mobility of a chest of drawers and he stared at me, no doubt wondering how to get me out of the bucket seat. He pulled and pulled and I finally fell out onto the pavement like the fat woman I was. I rolled around and finally got a foot under me. He hooked an arm under my free leg and with me hopping, and him dragging me, we got through the automatic doors, all the while he chanted his prayers.

I delivered immediately. The time of birth was recorded as 3:45pm. Forty-five minutes after my water broke. The intern who delivered the baby said it was a precipitous birth. He then shook hands with the guy shrinking in the corner of my room and said, "You have a beautiful baby girl."

"I'm not the father," he blurted.

If I'd been on my game I would have insisted he was. But sarcasm eluded me.

After a bit of confusion, I was able to give the nurse a number to reach Brian, then I quickly fell asleep.

We named her Elizabeth Ann. She was a beautiful baby.

CHAPTER EIGHTEEN

The Therapist

"Have you gone through any counseling before now?" she asked.

"No." I answered, surprised by her question.

"You've never talked with any professional about your stepfather, your mother, or how you got involved with Brian?"

"No."

There was a contemplative silence between us as she studied my face again. I had no idea what she was thinking.

"Were you a cutter?" she asked, then quickly rephrased the question. "Have you ever cut yourself?"

"No," I answered. It was a strange question, and I immediately searched my arms and hands for any scars that would have prompted her to ask it. There were none, except the odd nicks that come with age.

"I've had accidents, you know, like everyone does. But I've never purposefully cut myself if that's what you mean."

Silence filled the room again, but by now I was accustomed to waiting through it.

"I think you would have benefitted greatly from talking to a counselor after you left home," she finally said. "It's unfortunate that you didn't see someone."

More silence.

"And now you have a baby," she mused. Neither of us spoke for a few minutes, then she turned back to me and said, "Continue."

TEXAS

CHAPTER NINETEEN

J. H. Dunn Ranch

Brian and I moved our little family to Texas in 1974, when Beth was a year old. We actually set off the day after her first birthday. Brian was delighted at the thought of living in Texas, and I was looking forward to an adventure. We sold or gave away most of our possessions and packed the things we thought we absolutely needed into a small U-Haul trailer. Before we left California, Mom came to say goodbye, and whispered coarsely in my ear, "You're going to miss the mountains."

I had never been outside California, so it was unimaginable to me that other places might not have mountains or trees or the tepid weather I had grown up with. After four days on the road, I woke up to the car idling at a stop light, rocking violently as the wind blasted sand across a flat plain.

"Where are we?" I asked. It looked like a dusty version of Hell.

"We're here," Brian answered. He looked as astonished as I felt. There were no trees and no mountains. We were in Amarillo, Texas, and it was flat, dry, and windy. I was certain it was just a bad stop in the road.

We had come to Amarillo with the promise of a job for Brian working for my Uncle John, my Mom's youngest brother. Uncle John was managing a hog farm that was experimenting with feeds and techniques aimed at growing better pigs at a higher profit. I didn't think Brian was terribly interested in pigs, but jobs were scarce in California and he had been overjoyed at the chance to move to Texas.

As so often happens when you can least afford it, soon after we got settled into a rental house, I realized I was pregnant again.

I got a job working at a feed lot driving a dump truck. There were four drivers, each of us assigned an identical truck. We drove them in a line to the side of a cattle pen, where a toothless old man on a front-end loader filled each truck with cow flop. We then drove in a procession to the top of the only mountain in Amarillo, the largest pile of cow business in the tri-state area, and dumped our loads. We repeated the process all day long. One of the women who lived on the lot watched Beth while I worked. She was a sweet old woman who really enjoyed having a toddler around.

Within a couple of months Brian admitted he really didn't like working with pigs as much as he had anticipated and he quit his job. I wasn't surprised, nor overly concerned; Brian always managed to find work, and after taking a few temporary positions, he discovered his dream job as a working cowboy at the J. H. Dunn cattle ranch in Masterson, Texas.

The ranch was thirty-five sections, a total of about 22,000 acres. It had quite a colorful history as it was part of the original XIT Ranch that, back in its day, had covered 3,000,000 acres in ten counties of the Texas Panhandle. Brian was an extraordinarily happy guy.

I honestly don't know how Brian landed this cowboy job, as it had happened while I was in the hospital birthing our son. I delivered fast again, but fortunately Brian had been nearby and was able to drive me to the hospital himself. I chose the name Joseph Leo, after his grandfather Kenneth Leo, but was overruled. Adam Cole was the sweetest baby boy I could imagine.

At the end of September, 1974, when Adam was only five days old, we packed up our meager belongings and moved thirty-five miles due north of Amarillo to the J. H. Dunn Ranch. We were given an old ranch camp to live in, a rock house that was just that–boulders stacked on top of one another with a roof on top. It had no insulation but the chinking between the rocks kept the wind out and electricity had been added long after the structure was built so it ran in exposed pipe conduit along the inside walls. There was an addition of two bedrooms and a bathroom of stick frame and drywall, which modernized the home. It was truly an image of the last of the old wild-west. Brian and I loved it.

We only had one vehicle, a truck, and I became a stay-at-home mom with a 19-month-old daughter and a newborn. I didn't have a paying income, but I soon realized that going off the grid and living a self-sustained lifestyle required a lot of work. Wages for Brian's cowboying talents were only $500 a month. Other compensation included the house, utilities, a cow to milk, and a slaughtered steer every year. An old chicken coop was cleaned out and new chickens were installed. Up on the hill from the house was a fenced-in area that could be used as a vegetable garden in the spring. We had nearly everything we needed, but without a job I felt like I had checked out of the real world and had stepped backward in time.

The air gradually cooled from the typical West Texas summer heat. Electricity was dodgy at best, and brownouts were common. When I first told the foreman our electricity was out he said he'd have the men come fix it. I was surprised when Brian and another man turned up to repair the problem. I asked if either of them knew how to do electrical work.

"No," they both admitted sheepishly. But that didn't stop them from fiddling with the wires. I was amazed no one got electrocuted.

The ranch was beautiful. Not in the traditional sense of mountains and trees, but in the beauty that comes from a hard, weather-beaten landscape where things struggle to grow, and those that do, demand respect. Not much could have changed in hundreds of years. The roads were graded caliche, a sedimentary rock, a hardened natural cement of calcium carbonate that binds with other materials such as gravel. Most of the plains were of the same hard earth from which only the most stubborn buffalo grasses and scrawny mesquite trees grew. There were occasional flat-topped hills called mesas that rose up out of miles of plains, quite unlike the volcanic mountain range I had grown up near.

The plains were so flat I could watch storms build and roll in from miles away and the weather was always extreme. Hailstorms occasionally produced ice the size of golf balls. Snow rarely fell straight down; the wind almost always blew it into drifts eight and ten feet deep and it could rage for days. I hadn't particularly liked Amarillo when we first arrived, but I loved the primitive wildness of the ranch.

Cattle, horses, chickens, and all sorts of other farm animals were my companions in addition to the children. The nearest home was several miles away, and over the course of five years I only had occasion to meet the occupants once or twice, but I didn't mind the isolation. In fact, I relished it. I milked a cow morning and night, gathered eggs, grew a vegetable garden, kept a home, and played with the children. There was always plenty to do. We were almost self-sufficient between what I could grow and the free beef. I bought a milk pasteurizer and an electric butter churn, and I found an old treadle sewing machine that I learned to use. I cut material scraps from used clothing and made blankets and the kids' little clothes.

I was happy and content for the time being. On nice afternoons I could saddle up two horses, and with Adam in front of me and Beth on her own horse we would explore the gulches and meadows beyond our house. Sometimes we found Indian artifacts—an arrowhead or some beads. It was like being back in Rock Corral with Red, and I often thought about him as we rode.

Our mail was delivered to the Masterson General Store, located on I-40, a full five miles from our camp. I always timed grocery shopping with picking up the mail, a planned trip that took the better part of the day.

We were warned to keep our eyes open for rattlesnakes, but after not seeing any for a couple of months I had stopped worrying and just went about my business without thinking about them.

Anytime I made a trip into Amarillo, I collected cats from the ads in the newspaper. My theory was they would be useful in keeping the mice population under control, and in turn, the snakes would tend to go elsewhere for food. The cats led a good, if brief, life on the ranch considering they would have likely ended up being put to sleep at the animal shelter if I hadn't taken them. Unfortunately, their mortality rate was high at the ranch as well. Coyotes probably got a lot of them, and a couple of them killed themselves under the truck tires. But there was a never-ending supply of cats in Amarillo and people were always more than happy to have me carry them back for a nice life on the ranch. As a result, I never got to know any of them very well with one exception.

I picked up an old mud-colored cat with ears crumpled from frost bite who I named Horrible. She lived quite a long time and unlike a lot of feral cats I'd picked up, she always came to see me when I was at the barn. After milking the cow I filled several pans for all the cats, and they were welcome to catch as many mice as they wanted. Horrible must have been an excellent mouser, because we hardly saw any mice around during her reign.

One day the following April, I drove the truck up to the barn so the kids could sit inside while I fed the animals. As I returned to the truck I saw Beth waving wildly from inside the cab. Her little finger pointed at a giant snake slithering right in front of me as I was about to go through the gate. It was a rattler, and I had almost stepped on it.

I did a version of Yogi Bear in the cartoons when he's trying to get away from the Park Ranger. Adrenaline rocketed my body into the air, where my feet did an amazing bicycle spin that seemed to propel me backward, and when I landed, I'd managed to avoid stepping on the awful thing. It slithered on down the fence line without so much as noticing me. I ran to the truck and collected the shotgun Brian had insisted I carry, broke it open, and loaded two shells into it, then set about blasting away at the escaping snake. Every time I pulled the trigger I was knocked backward and pieces of snake meat and dirt rained down all around me. The snake's head and half its body struggled to keep moving, and as long as I saw it move, I kept reloading and shooting. I don't know how many shells I actually fired, but when I finally stopped, I couldn't find enough snake meat to spread on a cracker. Several small craters pocked the earth, and a whole pile of empty shotgun shells lay around me. That was the first of the many, many rattlesnakes I would come across on the Dunn Ranch.

It turned out I hadn't seen any snakes earlier because from October until April the weather was too cold for them to be out. They don't actually hibernate, but they do become "less active" during cold weather, and that particular winter had been especially cold. Once the ground started baking under the Texas sun, the snakes came out to party. Loads of them.

I discovered that just driving over a snake on the road would not kill it. In fact, the truck tires would actually bounce right on over it and the snake would wriggle on unscathed. Beth and I developed another method of eliminating the snakes we came across when we were in the truck, and we did it without firing a single shot.

Adam was just a baby, so he rode in a car seat in the middle of the truck cab. Beth was a two year old by then, and rode in a booster seat she was able to buckle and unbuckle as she pleased. It wasn't the most secure system for a kid, but that's what we had to work with. As soon as she or I spotted a snake in the road Beth would unbuckle herself and get into position riding shotgun by leaning slightly out the open passenger window. I increased the trucks speed, and when we were almost on top of the snake she would signal me with her arm, then brace herself while I slammed on the brakes. Hit just right the braked tires smeared a good track sized section of the snake's guts across the road and caused mortal damage, but it required a direct hit which took great skill. We became a good team. We always stopped and looked out the back window to see if the victim was wounded, and cheered when we had hit our mark.

If we were walking, we rarely ever came across a snake, but we chatted and carried sticks to beat the brush as we walked. We lost a good milk cow to snakebite, she was bit on the nose and her head had swollen to three times its size when we found her dead in the field. There were lots of coyote and antelope, but apart from the snakes, nothing really harmful.

The Dunn Ranch was an entirely different place to live; it was a world that seemed to have frozen in time. An escape from reality, it was a welcome respite from all that had gone on before. I saw it as a safe and easy place to watch the kids grow up. But I knew we couldn't stay there forever.

After we had lived on the ranch for more than a year I finally met Mr. Dunn. He was an incredibly interesting man. He liked his ranch, and when he escaped from his work in Amarillo, he drove his big land yacht Cadillac out to see how his cattle were doing.

I met him only a few times during the nearly five years we lived at the ranch, but he told me about being a paperboy when he was a kid, and running a hamburger stand to put himself through college. I told him I really wanted to go to college but it would have to wait, it was too far a commute, and the kids needed me at home right now. Mr. Dunn told me to look him up when I was ready to move off the ranch. He said he would help me get a job, and that I shouldn't give up on a college degree.

"You'll do it if you want to, if it's important to you," he said. I later learned that Mr. Dunn was chairman of the board of the Diamond Shamrock Corporation, an independent oil and gas company that headquartered in Amarillo. His success story encouraged me.

Brian loved his job for the first three years or so, but then his attitude began to change. He became frustrated. His co-worker was a single man and Brian began to resent having a wife and two children and the related responsibilities. He started spending more and more nights out hunting, or in Amarillo drinking beer. When I asked what was going on he became uncharacteristically angry and yelled at both me and the kids.

Beth and Adam were both easy kids, even as young as they were, and having grown up around horses and animals they were pretty savvy about being careful and always behaved well. But Brian avoided spending much time with them, he said, "...not until they are out of diapers." At the ranch, he had little time or patience for either of the children even after they were older.

Brian started bringing home copies of *Soldier of Fortune*, a magazine that advertised for mercenaries, and was eager to show me one with a picture of a camouflaged clad man holding up a decapitated human head.

"Why are you reading crap like that?" I asked as I threw the magazine back onto the table. "Do you want to be a mercenary now?"

Brian stood and grabbed me by the throat, and hissed in my ear, "Maybe. And if I want any shit out of you, I'll unscrew your head and dip it out with a ladle." Just as quickly he let go and went back to reading.

I was stunned. While I appreciated the originality of his comment, he had crossed a line. Brian had never put his hands on me in anger before.

Anger quickly replaced the shock. I wasn't a kid anymore and when I was tossed from The Property I had told myself I'd never let anyone hit me again. I put the kids into the truck and drove away from both Brian and the camp. As I drove toward the freeway I mentally assessed my situation. I had no money and no credit card, everything we bought we paid for in cash. I had no immediate way to get money. I had two toddlers and no family closer than 1,500 miles away. And, best of all, the truck was nearly out of gas. I drove back home and started planning how I could end this marriage and get on with my life.

I took the first job I found in Amarillo, at a meat-packing plant. It paid a whopping $4 an hour to cut meat from an assembly line. I located a woman who would watch both kids while I worked and when I asked Brian to take care of them on his days off to save money, he refused. It didn't take long to discover the reason. He had begun an affair with a friend of mine. That fact didn't bother me as much as I thought it would. My immediate concern was I needed to earn and hide enough cash to end this marriage. Brian shacking up with that cow made it was fairly easy, since he wasn't paying attention to what I was doing.

I skimmed money from both our checks each payday and when I had enough I opened a savings account in my name only. I alternated between making deposits to my account and stashing cash in a file in my closet. I didn't know if a lawyer would have to account for my savings in the divorce, and I needed to have an emergency fund in case I had to leave in a hurry.

Beth would be starting school soon, and I used that as the reason we needed to move off the ranch and back into Amarillo. After a year of cutting meat, my right wrist developed carpal tunnel syndrome, and when I found I couldn't hold a pen or write my name I had to look for other work. I had socked away a good chunk of dosh, and things were on track to make my break. With a bit of rest, my wrist recovered and I took a job at the local Sears store, as a collections clerk.

Brian continued to buy guns at an alarming rate. With my new income he bought big rifles with scopes, handguns, old guns, all sorts of guns, and all were added to his collection. To my knowledge, he never sold any of them. On his days off he would frequently take one or two guns apart and spread them all over the carpet, oiling each piece lovingly as he went. He used that as another excuse he couldn't take care of his children. They would get in the way of him cleaning his guns. His guns took additional guilt off me for hiding cash. We were both skimming from our paltry paychecks. It's a wonder we had ten cents left over.

Brian slowly accepted that we needed to move off the ranch, and we found a tiny two bedroom house for sale that fit us well enough. It was on the outskirts of Amarillo and cost $11,300 in the fall of 1979 and our payments were only $113 per month. I used a part of my hidden savings to purchase the place, and Brian applied for and was hired as a police officer with the Amarillo Police Department. Not long after, we moved up to a slightly larger home nearer the center of Amarillo, one that was close to an elementary school. By then I had replenished my savings and added even more.

As a police officer, Brian's ego got the better of him. He worked the swing shift, and many nights after work, he failed to come home. Most commonly he would arrive after the kids and I had left for school and work the following morning. After sleeping all day, he would repeat the cycle. The result was that we rarely ever saw him, which suited me. He came up with unoriginal excuses for his absences like, "I fell asleep watching TV in the lounge," or "I went to a cop party after work." But his absence from our lives let me prolong the inevitable, and save more money.

Brian ultimately began having relationships with women he had met while he worked, and these women began calling our home incessantly. Brian actually said to me as an explanation, "The best cops fuck anything that gets in front of them." I don't know how many other cops share that philosophy, but the enlightenment didn't do anything positive for our marriage.

I didn't wait much longer to divorce him. On January 2, 1981, I filed the paperwork. In retrospect, Brian wasn't a horrible guy; we were just kids ourselves, and neither of us really knew how to be married. We were 27 and 29 years old.

I wanted Brian to be responsible and pay child support, and I thought that something was better than nothing, so I set his payments at one hundred dollars per month for each child. Legally he would have been required to pay more, but I insisted it be set low. Still, Brian often found it difficult to pay, and he refused to pay through the court as they had required. However, without him spending our extra cash on guns and beer, we had more than enough money for the three of us even when he didn't pay the child support. I never increased it, and I never went after the back pay.

I never called Mr. Dunn either. I was stubborn and prideful I suppose, but I wanted to make a success of myself, on my own. Our divorce was final in April, 1981, and I was hired as a clerk in the Accounting Department of Diamond Shamrock in May, 1981, making $890 a month. I applied for the position and was hired with nobody's help.

Being employed at Diamond Shamrock was a turning point for me. It wasn't a great deal of money, but it was a really nice job and I was finally proud to tell people what I did for a living. I stayed there for the next ten years.

CHAPTER TWENTY

Diamond Shamrock

Getting a college degree had always been a personal goal. I grudgingly accepted that I wouldn't be a veterinarian, but beyond that I didn't have any real focus as to which degree I wanted.

When I discovered that Diamond Shamrock offered a very healthy tuition reimbursement plan I determined to take full advantage. I had never thought about accounting as a degree, but I had always been good with numbers and I was particularly interested in saving and investing, so I plotted to pursue a Bachelor's degree in finance. I enrolled at Amarillo Community College in a couple of night classes that fit around my work schedule.

The Diamond Shamrock Company headquarters were located in an old converted bank building in downtown Amarillo. Their stats boasted employing some 12,400 people in thirty-seven countries around the world in 1980, and I just added one more to that total. My cubicle was on the ground floor. It was the best job I'd ever had, and I followed Grandpas advice to do the very best I could.

But I was worried.

In early 1981 the Reagan administration deregulated oil prices. The result was an immediate and sharp increase in prices followed by a dramatic decrease. The market wreaked havoc on the oil and gas industry. Diamond Shamrock began downsizing to stall the hemorrhage almost as soon as I had been hired. The layoffs occurred every May, and they became known throughout the company as the Mother's Day Massacres. I survived the first of the many layoffs and gradually my pay and responsibilities increased. Within two years Diamond Shamrock merged with a company called Sigmor, and a major reorganization followed. The Oil and Gas, Refining and Marketing Department that I was working in, split from the parent company, and those operations were moved to San Antonio. This time I was one of the casualties.

I left the Human Resources meeting with my signed paperwork in hand, and descended the grand stairway toward the ground floor of the building. My movements were automatic. I couldn't recall a single word the six men had said. Although they had been gracious in their delivery, I knew I had been fired, and there's no gentle way to give someone that information.

At the bottom of the staircase, leaning against the handrail at the very last baluster was a man I knew as Fenton Farwell. He was a happy little Irishman who was blessed with a sharp sense of humor, and that day, with one ankle crossed over the other he looked every bit a leprechaun. He grinned up at me like I was his date for the prom.

"You got canned, didn't ya." he stated happily.

"Yeah," was all I could say, but his smile was infectious and I couldn't help but smile back. He watched me continue down the stairs.

"Tell you what." His eyes narrowed. "This is a one-time offer and it's only good for five seconds." He pointed up at me. "I'll hire you as an accountant right now, and give you a 25% raise. What's your answer?" I swear to God his eyes twinkled.

"YES. Really? YES!" I laughed, and briefly hoped that my five seconds weren't up. I hoped he really was in a position to hire me. I wondered if he knew I wasn't an accountant and only a clerk. And I hoped he wasn't making a fool of me.

"See Barbara upstairs and she'll get your office set up," he said. Then he waved his hand in the air and turned on his heel. He walked away with the happy, bouncy step of a true leprechaun. I stood watching him until he was no longer in sight. I half expected to see twinkly dust surround him.

Then I wondered if he knew my name.

Fenton Farwell most certainly was in a position to hire me. He was the assistant comptroller of Diamond Shamrock Company. He later told me that he had started at Diamond Shamrock as a clerk just as I had. He said he knew I was taking night classes and he expected me to continue going to school. I was given a private office with a door and a window, and beautiful furniture. Mr. Farwell was magic.

I handled the offshore gas wells accounting and tax payments for the next several years, a position that provided both an excellent income and the opportunity to learn. I was treated very well, and was competent in my work.

In April, 1986, I was promoted to Contract Administrator and was transferred to Dallas with the Exploration and Production Group. As part of the previous reorganization, Diamond Shamrock changed its name to Maxus Energy.

We moved from the desert dust bin that is Amarillo, Texas, to the suburbs of Dallas. It was a choice of moving 350 miles further east, along with a substantial raise and the new impressive title or be an unemployed single mom in Amarillo. It wasn't a choice at all. But my kids had to give up their friends, horses, and all but one of our dogs, and I felt guilty about that, so I bought a fixer-upper house with a pool in Plano, a city slightly north of Dallas, thinking it was a good trade-off for them. It was, but it was also an expensive one.

The pool didn't come with one of those cool creepy crawler things that constantly kept other people's pools clean, and never having owned or cared for a pool before, I found I was less than adept at managing the chlorine and muriatic acid and some of the dozen other things that a pool needs. As a result, the water invariably went from relatively clean and blue to suffocating in black algae in what seemed like a matter of hours. My kids were not interested in or effective at cleaning it, they only wanted to play in it. It became a real chore.

Everything about living in Plano was more expensive. The mortgage alone carried a 13.9 percent interest rate, which was the going rate at that time, but much more than my previous 5 percent, and the total payment was about double what I'd had in Amarillo. Utilities were more than expected, not to mention we now lived in a fairly upscale part of town, and the kids were getting older and needed more things. Their father had never been consistent with their child support, but even if he had been spot on time with it every month it wouldn't have paid for much. So, as any good accountant does, I cut back.

We got rid of the phone. It had become expensive, and was cut as a temporary measure. We got rid of cable and watched a very fuzzy small TV. We had never owned a VCR. We didn't eat out. We didn't have a home computer. We didn't have a pool service. I commuted by bus into downtown Dallas. We had a formal dining room for the first time ever, and I bought a wooden picnic table and benches at a garage sale for twenty dollars, which we installed under the sparkly chandelier. We bought day-old bread from the bakery, as well as ten-for-a-dollar snack cakes to include in our packed lunches. I repaired a leak in the ceiling of Adam's bedroom myself, and we painted and hung wallpaper on the weekends to update the glossy papers and colors that previous owners had chosen. The yard needed work but we could only mow the thin grass and pull weeds from the garden beds. We lived as cheaply as possible and got along just fine, and our finances slowly improved.

CHAPTER TWENTY-ONE

Rod

I met Rod almost a year after we'd moved, on January 18, 1987, at a church singles dance that I hadn't looked forward to attending. My daughter Beth, who was then thirteen, had grabbed the flyer from church and insisted all week that I should go. She selected the dress she thought I should wear from my closet, and the shoes, an ensemble that looked frighteningly like something out of the movie Dirty Dancing. That Saturday, she informed me that if after thirty minutes I wasn't having fun I could come home. Beth had always been a bossy little thing.

When I arrived at the dance I was grateful to see a bar. I settled onto a stool and ordered a rum and coke. Apparently it's just fine to get pissed out of your brain at church dances. I wouldn't know, I wasn't raised in church and that was the first and last church dance I ever attended.

Straight away I scanned the room for any men as tall as me. They're fairly easy to spot in a crowd and sometimes they run in pairs. But there was only one at this shindig, a dark-haired man who looked a bit like Herman Munster with a flat face and hands the size of skillets. He must have been looking for tall people too, because we locked eyes and he made his way over and asked me to dance. Great. We danced without touching and while he was busting his best moves, I noticed he was looking everywhere but at me. I danced pretty conservatively, which I always do unless I'm wildly drunk. I have no natural rhythm and am keenly aware that if unchecked, my arms tend to fly off in direct opposition to my feet. When the music stopped I thanked him and quickly retreated to my drink.

Back at the bar, a round, balding man of about 5'6" began chatting me up. His hands and shirt were sweaty, but he had a nice smile and he seemed friendly so I was happy to talk with him. He asked me to dance. I politely declined saying I needed to rest a bit. I was 34 years old and probably could have danced for hours – but I hadn't had near enough rum yet and this wasn't going to be one of those nights anyway. Just when I thought my half hour had to be up and I could go home, a very nice-looking man's head popped up above the crowd. The music ended and the group thinned enough that I could see he had been leaning over the hors d'oeuvre bar sniffing the cocktail weenies. I stifled a laugh as I watched him load a half dozen onto his plate.

I turned back to my drink and when I looked at the crowd again I could see the weenie sniffer making his way toward me. He was about 6' tall, give or take an inch. He was well dressed, attractive in a metrosexual sort of way, but when he stood beside me he didn't speak or look at me. Okay, so maybe he was only at the bar to order a drink. But he didn't order a drink, and after an obvious delay, he turned his attention toward me.

He bypassed the customary ritual of offering an introduction, instead, he dove right into interview mode, asking my name, age, marital status, number of children, workplace, house or apartment, etc. It was the strangest first meeting ever. I answered the first couple of questions but then got defensive because he wouldn't respond in kind and the interrogation felt intrusive. When I realized he wouldn't answer my questions with so much as his name, I turned back to my drink and ignored him. Unfazed, he turned on his heel and I watched him wander away.

What was that?

I stood up and put on my coat to leave when Herman Munster came back and asked for my phone number. I scribbled my first name and office phone number on a cocktail napkin, and left without another word. It wasn't that I was judiciously careful with my home number. For once I was happy I didn't have one.

The next Monday at work I got a phone call. The caller introduced himself as Rod and I recognized his voice from the dance.

"How did you get my number?"

He didn't answer, but said in a flat tone, "I'd advise you not to go out with Joe."

"Who the hell is Joe?" I asked.

"That's who you gave your phone number to at the dance, and I'd advise you not to go out with him," he stressed.

"Uh, yeah, I gave it to HIM – not to YOU. So why are YOU calling me?"

"He's not the right guy for you," he just wouldn't give up.

"Oh, and I suppose you are?" I shot back.

"Maybe. Let's meet and talk about it."

"No. I don't think so." I hung up.

Rod called once a day for the rest of that week and the next. His persistence was slightly flattering and he was just interesting enough that I got over my initial negative impression of him. I was taking a college night course in American History, and my assignment the following week was to watch the Oliver Stone movie *Platoon* and write a paper about it. I finally told Rod if he wanted to see me he could take me to that movie, but afterward I had things to do. It was sort of a date.

He picked me up and paid for both movie tickets, then bought a single box of popcorn. I assumed we'd share it, but when he handed it to me he stated, "You have to eat all of it." It was exactly the kind of off-kilter statement that would punctuate the rest of our relationship. Sort of a demand, sort of not, but one that just didn't seem quite right. I purposefully did not eat all of it.

He didn't call for a couple of days after that, which didn't bother me, but toward the end of the week he called again and asked if I wanted to meet him for ice cream at the weekend. *Good Lord, who IS this man? He could be anything from a sweet old-fashioned guy to an axe murderer.* I told myself this was why it's always better to meet men through friends. I knew nothing about him and had no one to ask. He may have just escaped from prison for all I knew. He might have been trying to be original, or maybe he was just frugal, and that possibility appealed to me.

That really may be the only reason I agreed to meet him that Saturday afternoon at Baskin Robbins. It was a cheap date, and I wanted to find out more about a guy who didn't try to impress me with money.

Over two scoops, he asked me what I was looking for. I didn't understand the question and vaguely thought *nuts and whipped cream might have been nice*, but held back on that answer. I figured he owed me something before I told any more about myself so I turned it back on him.

"I don't know, what are *you* looking for?"

"I want to find a nice woman about my age, get married, and have a couple of kids," he said just as calmly as if that rolls out of every man's mouth on a second date.

"Well, you need to keep looking," I laughed, "there are plenty of women who would just love to hear that, but I'm not one of them. I'm not having any more kids and I'm happy being by myself."

"For how long?" he asked quietly, still spooning his ice cream.

What? For how long what?

I was basically right off the ranch in West Texas, and maybe between that and my unsocialized childhood, our backgrounds were so vastly different that we just *seemed* to come from different planets.

"Where are you from?" I decided I needed some stats. He was almost too clean cut; he looked like he didn't even own a pair of jeans. Even his hands were softer than any man I had ever known. On closer inspection I noticed that his fingernails were in better shape than mine. I wondered if he was really a man. I wondered if he had a penis. Amused with the conversation in my head, I shot a look at his crotch. He wore Docker slacks that I calculated were baggy enough to conceal a penis.

"Iowa."

Well, I'll be damned. I'd never met anyone from Iowa before. Maybe they were all extra clean and a bit odd.

"How old are you?" I demanded.

"Thirty-four, same as you," he said, and anticipating my next question, "I was married once when I was eighteen years old. Divorced after less than two years. No children. I don't pay alimony or child support."

"How about your family?"

"What about my family?" he answered in rapid fire to my question.

I had to bite my tongue; I desperately wanted to ask if they paid child support. I decided to dial back that bit of humor.

"Mother and father still married? Number of siblings?" I asked instead. I might as well get the whole picture.

"Parents never divorced. I have five brothers, no sisters." He paused, "My mother is deceased."

"Oh, I'm sorry. Was that recent?" I asked.

"Couple of years ago," he explained, "colon cancer. Dad remarried. Anything else you want to know?"

"Nope, I was just curious."

The following week Rod called me at work again, and asked if I would give him my home phone number. He already knew where I lived, so I admitted that I didn't have a phone. There was a pause, then he said he worked with telephones and would bring one over.

"No," I said. I explained that I was sure a phone would look great hanging in that empty spot on the wall, but I didn't have a connection and didn't plan to get one so a phone would be useless.

The following day he called again and said he would install a home telephone for me and he would pay the bill.

"NO, thank you," I told him emphatically, "we're fine."

It *was* inconvenient not to have a phone. With the kids out of school at 3:00 pm and me not getting home until at least 6:00 pm, and some days having to rush right back out to school, there were times it seemed negligent not to have a way to call them. But I declined. I thought I had made that pretty clear.

But the following Saturday he brought over a telephone, and an answering machine. It turned out that with an address, anyone can sign up for phone service in their own name; it doesn't have to be the owner of the place. The kids were elated. The next weekend he ordered a VCR connection and hooked up cable to our tiny TV. Then he brought over a bigger TV.

I was wary. I didn't know anything about him. He didn't talk very much, and, when he did, his statements seemed odd. We hadn't slept together. Hell, he'd shown no romantic interest in me at all yet he continued to talk about marriage. The kids, however, were delighted.

I didn't want to remarry. But that didn't mean I didn't want to have a man around. My son was 12 and my daughter 13 years old, and especially at those ages I was *not* looking for a step-father for them.

There are things you need and things you want, and I'd have traded all the gadgets he had scuttled over in a heartbeat for a good lusty roll in the hay. But that didn't appear to be on Rod's agenda. I could only wonder what it was I didn't understand about men that this guy wasn't even remotely interested in me physically, but still wouldn't go away.

I never thought of myself as gorgeous in the way models or movie stars are, but I thought I was at least mildly attractive. I was tall and lean, but I didn't exude confidence in the way I carried myself or spoke. Having mastered being invisible as a kid I still dressed conservatively, not wanting to draw too much attention. I was afraid that my lack of higher education and being socially stunted was something healthy, normal men could smell on me like some grand stink. Maybe the only men I would ever meet were from the Mr. Make-Do, Mr. Right-Now, or Mr. Oh-give-him-a-chance camps. Maybe that was the best I could hope for.

I recall waiting uncomfortably in a plastic chair in a doctor's office with nothing other than a fish tank to entertain me, when I found a magazine. While leafing through it, I came across an article written by a psychologist who profoundly stated, "You'll never find anyone who is a perfect mate. The best you can expect to find is someone whose bad habits you can tolerate."

It struck me as a message meant specifically for me, and was a colossal disappointment. I discussed this with a well-meaning friend (also single) who said the psychologist was absolutely correct.

"But this guy, Rod...he's just strange," I complained.

She answered dismissively, "Yeah, yeah. They're all odd, they're men." She advised me to give him a second look.

I suppose I was ripe for bad man-picking. The author of that article couldn't have predicted that I would turn my life into a pretzel to accommodate someone whose faults I thought I could tolerate, but that's exactly what I did.

I have always been drawn to great couples, people who seem to have found their perfect mates. And why not–they're loads of fun to be around. But even as I mentally gave up looking for My Guy, my heart continued to want that kind of fun and closeness with someone.

And Rod kept showing up. He was just there. All the time. His car would be parked in front of my house when I got home from work, and he usually showed up uninvited on the weekends.

"Why did you give me a telephone? Would it be too much trouble for you to CALL and ask me if you can come over?"

Rod would look around sheepishly and ask, "Are you busy?" Then he'd smile. That tight-lipped, smug smile, obviously proud of himself.

Sadly, no. I wasn't busy. I decided I needed to change that.

And I tried. I made a date with a man I'd met in Dallas. When he brought me home Rod was sitting in my living room playing video games with my kids. Rod stood up like he owned the place, and shook hands with my date. I wilted on the spot, and never heard from that guy again.

I really tried to meet other men, but Rod was like a one-man Taliban. In those early years he wanted to go everywhere with me and I was flattered by that, but soon realized I had become as invisible to other men as if I wore a burka.

I found myself in a relationship with a man I didn't understand, but a man who was stealthily and certainly moving into my home and my life, and who left no room or time for me to meet anyone else.

CHAPTER TWENTY-TWO

The Jerk

"On a scale of one to ten, I'd say you're about a six and a half. Maybe a seven on a really good day." Rod was sitting at my kitchen table where we had been eating a lunch of sandwiches and chips. He picked up another chip and shoved it into his mouth.

"Six or seven, is that what you said?" I thought the look on my face would be enough, but he wasn't looking at my face. He was looking at his sandwich. I was as tense as a tuning fork, but tried not to let my voice give me away.

"Yeah. Six and a half," he repeated.

"And you said your ex-fiancé is a seven or eight?"

"Yeah."

"And your last girlfriend was an eight or nine?"

"Oh yeah, nine. She was a solid nine." He smiled admiringly.

I nodded, staring at him, waiting for any sign that maybe he was joking. He wasn't. He took another bite of his sandwich. Correction: He took another bite of MY sandwich. He sat in my house, eating my bread, my lettuce, my mayo, my lunch meat. If I'd had a brother, and he had said this, I probably would have laughed and punched his arm. But I didn't have a brother, and this idiot stick had been dating me for months, and he had just totally *insulted* me. Could he actually BE that dense?

In a flat, low tone I spit out the words, "Get out of my house."

He stopped chewing mid-bite and looked at me with surprise.

"Pick up all your shit and get out of my house. NOW!" I hadn't moved but the anger on my face had finally registered with him and he immediately dove into defense mode.

"You're mad? YOU'RE MAD?" He got up from his chair and screamed, standing over me, "Why the hell did you ask me that if you weren't going to like my answer?"

"Are you seriously going to stand there and act like that was a NORMAL thing to tell the girl you've been dating for the last six months? The girl you've been pressuring to marry you since our second date?"

My voice had steadily gone up a decibel. "Are you telling me you don't see ANYTHING WRONG with what you just said?"

He leaned dangerously close to my face, red and angry, eyes wide, and yelled, "*MAYBE LOOKS AREN'T EVERYTHING. MAYBE I LIKE YOU FOR OTHER REASONS–DID YOU EVER THINK OF THAT?*"

Oh, well, that's just fabulous. I feel so much better now, I thought to myself.

"You're a JERK. Get-out-of-my-house. NOW. And don't ever come back," I said in a steady voice. I held direct, unblinking eye contact with him so he could not mistake my meaning.

He swung his arm and cleared the table, then stormed out the door as he screamed, "YOU'RE CRAZY!"

I was so mad I was shaking. I stayed seated at the table and waited for my temper to cool, then got up and cleaned the dishes and food off the floor.

But he just never went away. He wasn't horrible, just a colossal jerk. A friend suggested I get a restraining order, but what would have been the basis–that he insulted me?

I was constantly confused by Rod. He could be sweet one minute and the next second I'd want to throttle him. Every compliment was tempered with a negative. He told me I looked great, then added that it was too bad my ankles were so thick. He sincerely congratulated me for being promoted at work, then said I should have asked for more of a raise. All gifts I bought him were immediately returned, "…so he could get something he really liked." When I became frustrated with the gifts giving, he started telling me a few weeks in advance of his birthday or Christmas what I should buy for him.

He took me out to dinner at my favorite restaurant in the mall, Tinos, on one of my birthdays. As we passed by a store window I showed him a dress I thought was beautiful. After dinner we went back by the store and Rod told me to try the dress on. They had it in size six and it fit me like a glove. It was absolutely gorgeous. Dark blue velvet with long sleeves and the neckline a set of mock jewels. I felt like a princess and twirled in front of the mirror. Rod told me to leave it on, and he paid for it. It was an expensive dress, and I was both surprised and pleased. But the next day he told me to return it. He said it was too expensive. Of course I couldn't take it back; the sales clerk had clearly watched me wear it out of the shop. Over the next few days Rod asked several times if I had returned the dress yet. I finally told him I wouldn't.

He chuckled, and never asked me again.

However, the kids liked him. He brought over pizza, taught Beth how to drive a car, and sometimes helped them with their homework.

I wondered if Rod was afraid if he built up my ego I would leave him. Maybe he was right. Bob and even Mom had been emotionally mean, but there was no physical violence in Rod's and my relationship and that was the line I had drawn for myself. I vowed I would call the police if I were ever hit again, and I would kill anyone who touched my kids, and had told him so.

I met a friend, a couple actually, who lived in the same neighborhood as Rod. Curt and LeAndra attended a party held one weekend night, in the greenspace between all the homes in that subdivision. Everyone brought a covered dish and their drink of choice. There were four couples present. Since they all lived within walking distance, no one worried about getting flat out drunk, so the booze flowed continuously. A couple of hours into the party, LeAndra stood up, and in a loud voice she asked the group, "What are the top ten things you should never discuss at a party?"

LeAndra looked around at everyone, then, barely able to contain her laughter she shouted, "Number One: Maaaa-sturbation!"

A moment of stunned silence followed, then I burst out laughing and nearly fell out of my lawn chair. Rod looked disgusted and turned away. The other couples giggled nervously. It was the funniest thing I'd ever heard anyone say. That single sentence was the beginning of a lifelong friendship. As we got to know them better, we found that Curt was not as boisterous as LeAndra, and was able to tolerate Rod's moods. The four of us got together nearly once a month for dinners, parties, and we even went on a few vacations together.

I accepted that Rod was just being Rod. Quirky, poorly socialized maybe, rude certainly, definitely odd, Rod. "A character" was how I politely described him to my friends and co-workers. And I tried to focus on his good qualities. He was exactly my age, he was attractive, and we looked great in pictures. He was a good provider. He came from a stable family. He didn't drink to excess, he wasn't a womanizer, he didn't gamble, and most of all, he wasn't abusive–he never hit me.

CHAPTER TWENTY-THREE

The Therapist

"What do you think attracted you to Rod?" she asked.

"He paid attention to me," I said. "Well, at least, at first he did. I guess I was flattered that he pursued me."

"There're all kinds of abuse besides being hit," she leaned back in her chair and cocked her head toward me.

"Yeah, I know." I nodded, and looked away. "But being a jerk isn't abuse. It just means he's a jerk, right?"

She said nothing, and the clock continued to tick in its steady rhythm.

She let the time pass as she stared at me.

The air was so still.

CHAPTER TWENTY-FOUR

Sam

There were continued layoffs at Maxus Energy and I was uneasy. I hadn't been able to complete my Accounting degree, even though I had continued to take classes. I had completed all the transferrable classes in accounting that the community college offered and had begun taking the core requirements. I found I was good enough at accounting, but I excelled in the English and Science classes. I began to wonder about a different career path.

One profession I considered was Nursing. From a purely rational perspective, it was a degree that would not be wasted. I would always be assured of finding a job, regardless of where I lived. It included the sciences I loved so much. I didn't know a thing about it other than from having been in the hospital twice myself, when I gave birth.

Each time I enrolled in another class, I checked to see if it was also required for Nursing. Finally, at the beginning of May 1991, I had reached an impasse. I had completed all the required basic classes, and would either need to quit Maxus Energy to pursue the Nursing clinical courses full time, or give up on that idea completely and enroll in the higher-level accounting courses.

I was spared the pain of making the decision: I was included in a layoff that very month. At the age of 38, I applied to Texas Woman's University as a full-time Nursing student. With the high grade point average I had maintained during my community college courses, I was quickly accepted.

Nobody in my family was surprised when I had gone into accounting. But everyone was very surprised when I went into nursing. There had never been a medical person in my family, not a single doctor or nurse. My Mom's youngest brother, my Uncle John, was a trained veterinarian, but I hadn't known him growing up.

I thought nursing was a rather close relative to being a veterinarian. Apparently the requisite education for looking after humans, when compared to that for animals, is far less complicated and expensive, and requires about half as long to finish the degree.

I loved school. It shouldn't have surprised me how much I enjoyed it: it's what I had wanted to do all my life. This time I really excelled at it.

The diseases and their treatments seemed like just so much common sense, and I was bewildered with those students who were stressed out by it. I audiotaped all my lectures so I could sit back and just listen, feeling my brain soak up the information. Upon arriving home I would immediately type up my notes, and then I offered copies to anyone who wanted them. They were very concise and thorough, having typed the lectures word for word from the tape. I've been told that copies of my notes are still being passed around by students at that university. I should have charged money for them.

I was told our instructors were grizzly, old Vietnam War veterans, and I knew that to be true for at least some of them. Tough as boots, I thought they were the best of the best and I admired and loved them dearly. I would have gone through fire if any one of them had given the order. A single word of praise from them was the highest of honors, and although they weren't liberal with it, they didn't hold it back when it was earned.

Study groups were fabulous fun. Setting the date, putting out the word, inviting anyone who wanted to come. The junk food: hot chocolate, cokes, garlic toast, pizza, wine, M&M's, anything and everything that was easy and horrible, and if it was greasy it was even better. Study group food was always, ALWAYS consumed down to the very last crumb; we ate like animals. That same practice is likely repeated year after year at every school around the world, but this was the first time for me and I didn't want it to end.

That feeling of belonging to something bigger was like a drug to me. We made charts of pharmaceuticals according to the diseases they treated, then created acronyms to help us remember them. Then flash cards were made and we quizzed each other. We laughed so much our sides hurt. I loved our study groups. It's no wonder I graduated with a 3.8 GPA, not the highest in our class, but one that I was proud of.

There was a pretty, young woman who only came to our study group once. At that time, about half of all the nursing students were in the 35-45-year-old age group, many of us starting a second career, but the rest were much younger, having known that they wanted to be nurses earlier in their lives.

Sam, short for Samantha, was among the young lot, probably in her mid-twenties. We had a couple of clinical rotations together, and it was easy to see she was very comfortable in her interactions with the patients. Beautiful, vivacious, and full of life, it was clear that Sam was going to be a great nurse.

The day after our study group I overheard Sam telling some of the girls that a man at her apartment complex was bothering her. When one of them asked how, Sam burst out laughing and explained she had turned him down for a date and now he was leaving notes on her car. "No big deal," she said, and changed the subject. I didn't think any more about it.

The lecture got started soon after, and we had a test coming up so we were focused on what may or may not be included.

A few days later I entered the main hall and could feel a current, a palpable tension in the air. We were all directed to a room near the front door of the university campus, and the dean and all the instructors were standing at the front of the room, facing us.

These women stood in too straight a line, heads up, shoulder to shoulder, eyes forward.

Something was wrong.

Once everyone had entered the room and found a chair, the tall, sturdy instructor, whom I affectionately called Horse, broke from the line of stoic soldiers and stood before us. With her back ramrod straight, the seemingly impossible words fell from her mouth: Sam had been killed the night before. Speaking at an even pace and with an incredibly strong voice, she paused just long enough to allow for the inevitable gasps, then proceeded in a cadence that caused my brain to snap back to the present as I strained to capture every unimaginable word.

"A man Sam had rebuffed saw her return from her date with another man last night. He knocked on her door and she opened it, probably thinking her date had forgotten something," Horse said.

"But it wasn't her date," she explained. "It was the other man, and he sliced her throat."

Horse paused again, cleared her throat, and continued.

"Even though Sam couldn't scream," she said, "there was evidence throughout her apartment that she put up a tremendous, valiant struggle with her attacker. A fight that left behind enough detail about the identity of the man so that the police had no trouble determining who he was."

One instructor in the line wiped her eye, but the others showed no emotion.

Horse slowly looked at each one of us, then straightened her back a fraction taller, and spoke the five haunting words I knew I would never, ever forget, *"We would expect nothing less."*

The silence was profound as she let that sink in. I was shattered, as was the entire class. But we were not allowed to sit and weep. Lectures would start in thirty minutes we were told, and routine made us pick up and move forward.

CHAPTER TWENTY-FIVE

Moved In

Life in nursing school was really fun for me. Unfortunately, I may have been having too much fun, as both Beth and Adam moved out of the house when they were in their late teens. They were not thrown out, nor did they run away. It was common knowledge in the Plano School District that emancipation was granted at age seventeen and most of the kids in Plano apparently saw that as a right rather than a threat.

But it was a shock to me that they both wanted to be on their own at such an early age, and I was devastated. I blamed myself, maybe if I had not gone back to school so late in life things would have been different. Neither of them had ever been beaten, nor abused in any way. I may not have been the very best, or the wealthiest mom, but I had kept them safe and always provided for them.

I told them it was going to be hard, they would have to work, pay their own bills, and I worried about school. I had always encouraged them both to go to college. But my fears and warnings fell on deaf ears. They moved out.

By late that summer of 1991, it was apparent neither Beth nor Adam would be coming back home, and I found myself without children for the first time in my adult life. I was lonely, and I suppose that's the main reason I accepted Rod's offer to move in with him. I paid half the mortgage on his house and had no other expenses. My car was paid for, and I got a job with flexible hours at a nearby steakhouse.

I had never waited tables before, but discovered I really enjoyed the people and the work and particularly the subsequent payoff in tips. I was amazed how much money people left. I had never been able to leave much more than the bill myself, and typically avoided eating anyplace tips were expected. In my mind, people who left healthy bonuses were rich folk who could afford the extravagance. I soon happily discovered that a vast amount of people were apparently wealthy enough to part with what I considered to be a very healthy tip.

I worked most of the dinner shifts during the week and easily made enough cash to put gas in the car and have pocket change. My student loans, yearly grants, and all the scholarship cash paid my bills and college fees. Most of the nursing students only applied for the big scholarships, ignoring the $100–$500 offerings. I applied for every scholarship I qualified for and won a lot of the small ones and a couple of medium-sized ones too.

Between work, school, study, and sleep, Rod and I rarely saw each other. I was surprised how much I could fit into a day, and sometimes I wondered what I would do when I graduated and only worked a forty-hour job. Would Rod and I get along being around each other so much? Doubtful.

Living with Rod was certainly an adjustment. Rod's house was decorated like a dorm room, if dorm rooms resemble cluttered prison cells with lots of electronics. He had a cinder block bookshelf that held his stereo system, his big giant screen television crammed into a 14'x14' living room that required us to sit so close that we couldn't see the whole picture at once, and of course, a roommate.

Fortunately, the roommate was a nineteen-year-old college student who lived downstairs. He moved out when he graduated the following year.

Rod had rules. Lots of rules.

Rule number one: No one was allowed to use the stove or oven. No problem there, I was hardly a culinary wizard. My kitchen skills were more along the lines of a sandwich aficionado and I wasn't home much of the time anyway.

Rule number two: Each person was responsible for their own laundry. This rule was instituted shortly after I accidentally shrunk a pair of Rod's pants two sizes and dyed all his underpants pink. Oops.

But Rod took it a step further. I wasn't allowed to touch his laundry. He took his pants and shirts to the dry cleaners, and laundered his own undies. It seemed odd to me, but it certainly wasn't something I was going to complain about.

Rule number three: Spills had to be wiped up with a paper towel, not a fabric kitchen cloth or sponge. This was a vital rule, and Rod wouldn't explain why it was so critical. But the rare instances that I did grab a sponge to swab up a drip always earned me some unpleasant yelling time.

Rule number four: No furniture could be brought into the house unless it was purchased by Rod. He had to own everything in the house. Everything. I had recently purchased a new washing machine and dryer, but was told I had to sell them before moving in, even though Rod's washer and dryer were quite old. I decided he was just being careful, in case I didn't stay.

Rule number five: Shower times were assigned and strictly adhered to. Nobody wanted to be the one accused of using up all the hot water when The King finally rolled out of bed in the morning and wandered into the bathroom.

Rule number six: Each of us was assigned a shelf in the refrigerator for our own food.

None of his rules were deal breakers, by any means. I was quite happy not being responsible for any cooking or laundry. But I didn't understand why he was so rigid and demanding. I thought his rules were funny, and didn't take them too seriously.

It didn't take long to discover that Rod had food quirks too. On an average day he ate large quantities of plain bagels, raw almonds, and ginger ale. Sometimes, nothing else. He kept at least twenty cases of ginger ale stacked in his workout room lest he run short, and he bought his bagels and almonds in such bulk quantities that his stuff began showing up on my shelf in the refrigerator as well as his own.

"I see you're encroaching on my shelf," I joked as I looked in the fridge. I only kept a tub of margarine and occasionally a candy bar or two, and maybe some fruit.

"It's not like you're using it," Rod said defensively.

"You were supposed to laugh," I countered.

"I didn't think it was funny," Rod answered, giving me the stink eye.

I guess I had my own food quirks too. I ate at the restaurant salad bar most nights, and I always took a peanut butter sandwich to school in my bag, as a result, I didn't keep many groceries at home.

Rod would eat out on occasion, but would always, ALWAYS change his order. He never ordered his meal as it was described on the menu. If it came with mixed vegetables, he would ask for rice instead. If they said okay to the rice, he would ask for fried rice, or saffron, or basmati rice. If they couldn't comply with his order, he would start all over with another selection. He ordered blackened chicken without the seasoning. He ordered grilled tuna without the grill marks. And once it arrived, at least a third of the time he would send it back. Ordering off a menu took forever, and was embarrassing for anyone at the table with him.

"Jeez, why don't you go home and have a bagel," I once asked.

"I'm the customer," he proudly explained. "The customer is always right."

I figured he could be as odd as he wanted to be, as long as we were just roommates, but Rod still wanted to get married and brought up the subject often. My biggest problem was that I never believed Rod really loved me. That was sort of okay, because I knew I didn't really love him either. We tolerated each other and I thought I had learned how to get along with him. And we did care for each other. Eventually we even said the L-word, although I think we both understood it to be a better description of caring, rather than any deeper feelings.

Ours was definitely not the kind of love songs are written about.

That deep emotionally bonding kind of love, where couples have similar tastes, and are so in-sync with each other and laugh together and have private jokes–that was something

I'd only seen in a few couples, and read about in books. I was resigned to the fact that the majority of people never experience that type of love, and I was one of the majority.

Rod wasn't embarrassed of me; he always wanted me to go to Iowa with him to visit his family, and he even seemed quite proud to take me to his 20-year high school reunion. But he came with me to California to see my family only once and he declared he would never do it again, even though he had a good time. He refused to go with me to my Grandmother's funeral, or any other family visits, and wouldn't reciprocate when it came time for my 20-year high school reunion.

I hadn't attended any of my class' yearly reunions, and I hadn't particularly wanted to go to my 20th. But after going to Rod's, I began to look forward to my own. When he refused to go with me, I went alone.

As expected, I didn't know very many people at the reunion, but I remembered seeing some of them at school. It was entertaining to see how some classmates had changed over time; some had improved from their teenage years, others fared worse.

There was a table at the front of the room that displayed several of the school's yearbooks, from the years I had attended. I had only purchased a yearbook my first year, but hadn't been able to afford the others. I leisurely flipped through the second book when something caught my eye and I went back a couple of pages.

It was a picture of my counselor. He was wearing a suit and tie. He was smiling. But there was something else. Something so familiar, yet I couldn't grasp what it was, something about his face and his eyes. He had been so kind to me and I thought of all he had done to help me. I closed the book and set it back on the table. I had just began to walk away when it hit me. I stopped in mid stride. *No way,* I thought, *it couldn't be.*

I hurried back to the table and found that page again, and stared at his picture. I held my hand sideways over his forehead.

Recognition stopped me cold.

He was the same man who had helped me find a pasture for Red all those years ago.

My skin prickled and I covered my mouth with my hand. I couldn't look away from his picture. All the times I'd seen him flashed like a movie in my head. In his driveway, wearing the ball cap. Looking at me with his eyes scrunched up. Driving me home, when I'd slept. At Mr. Rush's, showing me the pasture. Why hadn't I connected the dots years ago? But of course, he had helped me with Red when I was 13, and I didn't start high school until a year later. I recalled the times I'd met with him in his office, never really making eye contact. Getting me out of school. Driving me to live with Terry. How much he had done for me; he had rescued me in so many ways.

I had never asked his name back then. And I had never known my counselors name. Looking at that picture, I knew those two men had to be one and the same person.

CHAPTER TWENTY-SIX

The Will

The summer of 1991, Rod and I had been dating for four years when he decided we should write our wills. I didn't own anything worth assigning to anyone and had never before considered writing a will. The coin collection I'd saved with Grandpa was valuable only to me and not worth much even at melt price. The only other nice thing I owned was a small collection of Victoria's Secret bras and panties. Not the kind of stuff that requires litigation.

But Rod was adamant. He had purchased computer software to write his will and he insisted I use it to create one at the same time. We sat down one night with a glass of wine, and I joked through every clause as I filled in the blanks of my document. I had nothing but some school loans and a beat-up car, and I happily left everything to Rod. He owned a mortgage on a house, a nice BMW car, a big screen TV, and a small 401 (k) savings account, plus a reasonable amount of debt. I was flattered when he named me as his sole beneficiary.

He wrote in a special section that he wanted to be cremated, and did not want a funeral. He added space and wrote the words he wanted to have printed on a Memorial Card to be distributed to his family and friends upon his death.

I agreed cremation was fine and I didn't have any particular interest in cards or funerals, but I wrote that my ashes should be sprinkled over Disney Land. It was a fun evening.

Rod had both copies notarized and witnessed the following day.

The papers were filed away and I forgot all about them.

CHAPTER TWENTY-SEVEN

Depression

I graduated *Summa Cum Laude* in May 1993 with a Bachelor of Science in Nursing. It was an exceptional day for me, and the people who came to Texas to celebrate my graduation all behaved themselves.

Mom flew in from California, and gave me a watch, one with a second hand so I could use it for work. Bob came too, and surprised me with a $5,000 deposit in a bond fund. He even told me he was proud of my accomplishment. That was the only time he ever said he was proud of something I had done.

Rod gave me luggage, nice leather stuff, inside which he had hidden $300 in one dollar bills.

I was the first college graduate in my family and I'd done it all on my own, though I had over $20,000 in student loans to pay off, so I still had a lot of "doing it on my own" left. It was a really good day, definitely one of the best days of my life. The school I had graduated from and my impending diploma had already landed me a critical care internship in a large hospital nearby.

Rod and I got married in Hawaii, on January 18, 1996, exactly nine years after we had met at that church dance. We didn't invite anyone to go with us; it was a private ceremony on the beach. The night before, I told Rod I would only go through with the ceremony if he could finally convince me he really loved me. It was a last ditch effort. I'm not sure what I expected.

"Oh course I love you," he answered flippantly. "I do. If you don't believe me, you're looking for something that doesn't exist."

When I didn't answer he added, "You've been watching too many LifeTime movies. What we have is normal. Your problem is you don't know what normal is."

He had a point. I wasn't sure I'd recognize normal if it fell from heaven, but I knew without a doubt that *he* didn't really love me. He was lying. *El es mentiroso.* His pants were on fire, his nose was growing. In every way I could say it, he was lying.

I had spent way too many brain cells trying to determine whether it was Rod or me that wasn't quite right. He was from a hardworking Danish family in Iowa, the third of six brothers, all of whom seemed to be quite stable and happily raising families, and his parents had never divorced. On paper, at least, he looked like he should know what normal is. By comparison, my stats didn't look so good.

This is the life I've got, I thought to myself, *other people are lucky in life, some are lucky in love. I'm one of the majority who just finds someone whose faults I can tolerate.*

I could have moved to another state. I could have looked for another man. I had my degree, made my own money, I could go anywhere I wanted. But I always had my doubts.

Another man might be so much worse. I was too afraid of the unknown to make a change. I held tight to the financial security that both our incomes provided.

So we married.

Rod and I built a house together in Plano. It was a spec home, but nonetheless, we purchased it together. I was against buying the house at first. It was enormously big. Four bedrooms, three full bathrooms, three living areas, three garages, a huge kitchen. Honest to God, what do two people do with that much space? I was embarrassed of its pretentious glamour. But Rod had plans for each and every room. Big screen over here, workout gym in the downstairs bedroom, and another bedroom for a home office so he could telecommute. I gave in. He made the big money and I guessed he should get a bigger vote deciding how to spend it.

Throughout our marriage I was invariably asked how Rod and I ended up together and, more importantly, why we had stayed together for so many years. Believe me, I asked myself that same question time and again. The honest truth may be, I think, I was lazy. Or challenged. Though not challenged in the way someone suffers a disability, challenged as in an act of defiance. Or maybe both lazy and challenged, although those seem to be competing elements. However, the biggest reason was that there didn't seem to be a good enough reason to leave him.

Once we were legally married, there were a few changes I hadn't expected. First, Rod wanted to eliminate my bank account and commingle our money. I had managed my own money all my life, and he had never mentioned this in the entire nine years we had dated. I held off and we argued about it for more than six months, until I gave in and Rod took control of my finances. It was a crushing defeat and one I regretted the second I agreed to it. Although Rod proved to be competent at paying bills on time, he had his thumb on me now, and he questioned every purchase I made.

The other change was more subtle. Even though he still refused to go with me to California, now when I went back to visit, he called as soon as my plane landed, asked what I was doing and who I was with and when I would be back, even if I had just told him. After just a few days he would begin pressuring me to change my flights and come home early.

Oddly, he didn't mind when I wanted to hike with the Sierra Club. I went to Glacier National Park in Montana and the Grand Canyon in Arizona, and he happily drove me to the airport for those backpacking trips, but he refused to go with me. Even more hurtful, he didn't want to hear about my adventures when I returned.

He became arrogant in his criticism of the books I read.

"I never waste my time reading fiction," he stated derisively, "I only read business magazines."

Really? I thought. *So that porno stash I found in your office closet is full of stock tips?*

There were times when we met in the hall and he would purposely move sideways so he wouldn't touch me. It was common when we were walking outside, for him to cross a street without me. He never, ever held my hand. There were so many little things that though individually insignificant, they added up over the years, and became extremely oppressive.

As a result, we cobbled together an existence that only required a minimum amount of contact with each other.

Beginning in the morning, I got up at six o'clock and left for work at seven, while Rod stayed in bed until after I'd left, presumably going to work around nine. I came home between six or seven in the evening, played with my two sheltie dogs for a while, at times went for a run, and was in bed by nine o'clock. Rod stayed up watching television (news and sports only of course) until about one in the morning, when we would switch places. I got up and played on the computer for a few hours, and returned to bed usually around three or four, before repeating the routine all over again.

Out of the 24 hours in a day, the total time we spent together was approximately two hours–sleeping.

Weekends were similar. We kept the same sleep pattern as the weekdays, except Rod laid in bed watching cartoons or a news channel until noon. When he finally got up he'd put on his unwashed, smelly gym clothes, and work out until early evening. After a shower, if I was home, he would ask if I wanted to go out to eat.

Meanwhile, I filled my Saturdays and Sundays shopping or working an extra shift at the hospital or sometimes getting together with friends.

Rod had always yelled at me, nearly from the time I met him. Not continuously, but certainly often. Sometimes I'd broken a rule but sometimes there was no reason for his outbursts whatsoever. But there came a time shortly after we married when he couldn't speak to me at all without yelling.

"Why are you always yelling at me?" I asked him.

"I'M NOT YELLING!" he would answer. "WHY DO YOU ALWAYS SAY ALWAYS, AND NEVER? YOU ALWAYS SAY I YELL, AND THAT I NEVER DO ANYTHING NICE–YOU NEED TO STOP SAYING ALWAYS

AND NEVER, KAAATH-EE. IT REALLY PISSES ME OFF."

"Do you talk to everyone like this? This, this...*not* yelling? The people you work with...do you talk to them like this? Or do you reserve it as a special treat just for me?" I asked.

"I'M NOT YELLING, KAATH-EE," he would scream back at me.

Well, I'm not deaf, I thought to myself, *and that sounds an awful lot like yelling to me.*

One evening when he started berating me as usual, with his face twisted and red, spewing his usual nonsense, I turned on my school tape recorder and set it down in front of him.

"WHAT'S THAT, KAATH-EE? YOU THINK YOU'RE SO GODAMN SMART," he was livid, spitting, and trembling; he was so mad.

"This is a tape recorder. You don't think you yell at me and I think you do. Obviously, we have a difference of opinion. I'm going to record you and we can play it back so you can hear what I hear." I laid it down and hit play.

I was pretty immune to Rod yelling at me and I was vaguely amused by it. I had learned not to listen too closely or I'd start laughing. Laughing never went over well. Rod did not appreciate my humor.

Regardless of how many times I explained to Rod that talking was a much better way to communicate with me, he never understood.

For a few seconds, after I started the recording, nothing happened.

Then Rod leaned forward in his chair and began spewing anger in a fairly controlled voice, and quickly worked himself up until he was again yelling at me in what had become his normal volume. He ranted for a good twenty minutes.

A couple of hours later, I rewound the tape and played it back for him. His face went white, he looked absolutely ashen. He switched the recorder off after only a few minutes. He looked really shocked. I think he must have honestly believed he *hadn't* been yelling.

And he never yelled at me again, but I paid a hefty price for that pleasure.

When he stopped yelling, he almost completely stopped speaking to me as well. The only time I could depend on having a two-way conversation with him was when someone else was present. Our home was certainly a more peaceful place, but it became terribly, terribly lonely.

We existed like that for years. To begin with, I thought it was sustainable. I had gotten what I wanted; he wasn't yelling anymore. But as the years rolled by and my loneliness grew, I finally realized that this was not a life I could tolerate. I tried to adapt by becoming a workaholic. I worked two, sometimes three jobs at a time. I did anything I could to stay out of the house and be around conversational adults. But sooner or later I would have to go home, and home was the saddest place in the world.

I got fat. I didn't think of myself as fat, but the scales gradually added a pound and then another pound or two, until my clothes didn't fit the way they used to. It took a few years, but I packed on a good solid thirty-five extra pounds. I still didn't think I was fat, but pictures don't lie; the girl in the group photo on dress-up day at work, who was standing in my spot–*she* was definitely fat.

I hated myself. I quit showering. I hated what I looked like in the mirror. I was old and fat and worse, I looked sad. I stopped calling my friends. I didn't care about anything; I was just following the daily routine, going through the most basic of human necessities, and cell by cell I could feel myself slowly dying. Then I almost lost myself completely.

One day in August 2000, I woke up at my usual time of about one in the morning, when Rod had come to bed. As I sat down at the computer I looked at my reflection in the darkened screen. I stared at the image for several seconds and suddenly everything that had been holding me together started to break apart bit by bit, like pearls from a broken string hitting the floor one by one. I started crying. I was still crying six hours later when I should have been getting ready for work, and I knew I couldn't stop. I was totally undone. I could barely punch in the numbers as I called my daughter.

We talked for just a few minutes, then she drove me straight to the emergency room. I felt drained, like there was nothing left of me. I had never felt so worthless. I was seen by an Indian doctor whose name tag said Dr. Saad, and that brought fresh tears. I was labeled with severe depressive disorder, and he traded my clothes for sandpaper scrubs then shipped me via police car to the local mental hospital. I cried all the way there.

After processing I was assigned a small room with a cot, given some sort of medication, after which I slept for the next 22 hours. A nurse finally woke me, saying a doctor was there to talk with me.

I found him sitting in a closet-sized conference room, sifting through a file which I assumed was mine.

After introducing himself, he asked how I was feeling. The blackness returned and I began crying again, laying my head on my arms. He waited.

"I've started you on Zoloft, which is an anti-depressant. It may take up to two weeks to become effective as it works on your neuronal uptake, blah, blah, blah, dopamine something-something, and the problem with that is you may have to stay here until it takes effect." He spoke in a made-for-television quiet voice that I imagined he reserved for crazy people.

Only a few of his words had registered with me.

Two weeks, I thought, *bloody hell*. I slowly raised my head and tried to look at him.

"Do you want to tell me what happened?" he asked.

I told him I was just lonely, and I couldn't stand it, and I had just started crying and didn't stop.

"I'm so lonely I just want to poke my eyes out," I wailed.

"So your husband travels for his job? He's away a lot?" he guessed.

I lost it again. "Nooooo, he's there (sniff) *ALL* the time." I dropped my head back down on my arms and sobbed. This guy just didn't get it.

Dr. Shrink waited, then asked, "You tried to kill yourself, didn't you?" He sounded skeptical, like I had conveniently left out the good part of the story.

"NOOoooo.... I just...can't-stop-crying."

He put his pen down and turned his chair to look directly at me. "Did you have a *plan* to kill yourself?"

"No," I wished he would just leave me alone so I could go back to bed. Dr. Shrink pushed a box of hospital tissues toward me that were so thin they disintegrated with one blast from my nose. I probably had bits of tissue stuck all over my face. I didn't care. I heard him huff, then he looked back at my file, slammed it shut and stood up. The crying had slowed again. I had progressed to sniffle and jerk mode.

"Well, if you didn't have any intention of killing yourself, why were you brought here?" he asked with a little irritation in his voice.

"I don't know. I got Dr. Saad," I said, as if that should clear everything up. "He talked to me in the hospital, then said I had to go in the police car."

I started crying again at the mention of Saad, and blew snot as I sobbed. Looking up, I wiped an entire handful of the see-through tissues around my face. They turned into the texture of a chunk of shredded wheat.

They really should provide a decent tissue for the emotional upsets in here, I thought, *I can't be the only one crying.* That made me cry too.

"Dr. Saad?" He repeated, almost laughing, then quickly turned away from me and reopened my chart. I was sure he saw it was all signed by one big-ole Dr. Saad. This time I didn't need to make up a nickname.

Dr. Shrink stood up again and bolted from the room.

He returned after a few minutes and, with his head stuck through the door, told me he would write prescriptions for an anti-depressant and another for Xanax to help me sleep and I was to come back and see him in a week. I was released a couple of hours later.

The Zoloft was magic; I stopped crying by the time I left the nut house, progressed quickly, and never had another bad day. I was back to my old self of finding life funny within just a few days. Pilled to the stratosphere I felt so good that I wondered how I would ever know when I could stop taking the drugs. After I'd been seeing Dr. Shrink a reasonable length of time, I asked that question, and he said I needed to take the medication for a full year, then "we" could try stopping them.

A condition of my continuing on the magic medication was to see a therapist once a week for an hour. That sounded like pure luxury, really. This would be an adult who *wanted* to talk to me? Someone who wouldn't get bored, change the subject, or run away. What wasn't to like? Okay, this would be a paid friend, but no wonder people stay in therapy for years and years. I was nervous but excited to get started.

After I'd been seeing the therapist for a couple of weeks, Rod broke down and spoke to me. He wanted to know what I was saying in therapy. Specifically, he wanted to know what I'd said about him.

"Oh no, I'm sorry. That's confidential. But yeah, it's all about you, that's all we talk about," I said. Sarcasm was back in good supply as well as my humor. I didn't care if Rod understood it was a joke or not.

Insurance paid a large portion of those visits but there was an out-of-pocket cost, and after about six months Rod said he thought I'd had enough therapy and needed to quit. I refused, and continued seeing her for an additional six months despite his objections.

By then, I was in the process of buying another house.

I had been visiting a friend out in Rockwall, Texas, near Lake Ray Hubbard, when I saw a row of apartments that bordered the lake, just beyond the I-30 Bridge. Upon closer inspection, these were a row of smallish, two bedroom townhouses that shared common walls on two sides, with the fronts facing a street and the backs open to the lake. With a little more investigation, I found they were quite affordable.

I learned that Lake Ray Hubbard was a man-made lake, and was built by the City of Dallas to serve as an emergency water supply. They had originally planned to remove all the trees from the lake bed before it was filled, but obviously they neglected to get the ones in the part of the lake that sat right behind these townhomes. The view was sort of ghetto fabulous, but that was probably what had kept the prices down. Regardless of the tree stumps, it was a lake, and these homes were right on the water's edge.

There were three currently for sale.

Unfortunately, the realtor I had contacted called and Rod answered the phone before I could get it. Even though I'd told her to talk only to me, she happily asked him to confirm the date and time of our viewing. *Freaking fantastic.* I had been passively plotting to leave Rod. I felt great, and I worried if I didn't leave him now while I had the help of my pharmaceutical crutches, I might slip back into the yuck pit I'd just climbed out of.

I really, really didn't want a big confrontation and I had stupidly thought Rod would ignore me in his usual manner, and I could just quietly buy a house and move in before he even noticed I'd left. That didn't go quite as I had imagined. I realized I needed to be honest about what I wanted.

So, I toughened up and told Rod I wanted a divorce. I said he could keep the big house we were living in, and all the stuff in it. I would be happy with this tiny place at the lake. There was a hospital nearby and I was certain I could work there.

Surprisingly, Rod begged me to stay. Begged like his life depended on me staying.

"Why?" I asked. "You don't even talk to me. We don't have a marriage–we just happen to have the same address."

Still he begged. He insisted nothing was wrong.

I thought if Rod would see one of these paid talking friends, he might be made to understand how wrong we were for each other. I suggested, but Rod quickly rejected seeing a marriage counselor.

He just literally begged me not to leave. Ultimately, I gave in. He was groveling and pleading, and I couldn't stand to see it. So I backed off demanding a divorce, for the time being. But I held fast to the lake house. Like breathing air, somehow deep in the marrow of my bones I knew I needed to buy it.

One of the townhomes was adorable. It needed paint, new flooring, new windows, new air conditioning, updating, and much, much more, and it was priced slightly higher than it was worth. But I loved it. I paid a deposit and signed a contract.

Rod was furious.

He told me the place wasn't worth what I'd offered. *I didn't care.*

He said it wasn't big enough. *It's big enough for me.*

It didn't have a garage, or room for his workout equipment, or his big screen TV. *Good,* I thought, *I don't want those things.*

He seethed through every meeting with the realtor and during our closing. He insisted I list him as a co-buyer so I had his name added to the contract. But when he discovered my name was listed in front of his on the title, he went ballistic and nearly refused to sign. In front of the very nervous realtor and closing agent I told Rod he didn't have to sign, that I was more than happy to purchase the place in my name alone. The room was thick with tension. He finally signed and I got the keys to the place on August 30, 2001.

I spent nearly every weekend at the lake house. I always had a project to work on. I never spent a ton of money, and I did most of the work myself. Eventually I hired a handyman to do the bigger projects like laying the floor tiles and replacing the air conditioner. I furnished the place with second hand stuff I found at garage sales or on eBay. It was the most awesome house and I loved being there in my tiny space.

After several months, I noticed my weight was decreasing. Within a year, I was back to my former size. I looked better, felt better, and was much happier. I stopped taking the Zoloft, and I was fine.

I bought a blow-up canoe and paddled myself around the lake until it sprung a leak. I nearly drowned myself laughing as I paddled frantically back to shore in the fast-sinking floatie. I had parties with co-workers on the deck overlooking the lake. Friends dropped over. I cooked when I wanted to. There was no internet connection so I slept all night. I gardened. I played loud music. I felt grown up and in charge of myself for the first time in my life.

LeAndra came to the lake house one weekend and we talked about recent events, as we always did. After I'd explained what had been going on, she said she never thought Rod and I would stay together forever. She said we were just too different, that I was far more social than he ever wanted to be, and she believed eventually I would divorce him. It was almost as if she gave me permission. I still wanted to divorce, but I just wasn't strong enough to demand it.

Rod only came to the lake house on occasional Saturday nights, and he would typically leave the following Sunday morning. He let me know he didn't enjoy staying in what he called "The Shanty." He nearly stopped coming out altogether.

However, he never seemed bothered that I spent most of my free time there.

CHAPTER TWENTY-EIGHT

The Therapist

"I think it's time we end our sessions," the therapist stated.

It felt like a very abrupt ending to me.

I panicked. "Why? What did I say?" I instantly thought she was angry with me. I don't know why I jumped to that conclusion, but why else would she want to end now?

"Nothing's wrong. I just feel that we've covered a lot of territory, you're up to the present, and as we've discussed, you can see the patterns of abandonment and abuse in your childhood now. It's time to let those things go now, and move on with your life."

I thought about that. It didn't feel like a normal conclusion to a doctor-patient relationship, but then I'd never seen a therapist before so I concluded this must be the natural ending.

"I'm sorry, I guess I've just gotten used to coming in here every week, and I wasn't expecting it to stop just yet. But yeah, uh, I guess there's nothing else to talk about."

I suppose she was satisfied I wasn't suicidal, and could document that in her notes, so our sessions ended.

Rod and I continued living semi-apart in the two houses off and on for the next seven years. Since we almost never saw each other, we got along quite well. We "almost" lived separate lives. It would have been perfect, had it not been for Nortel's failing business and the deteriorating economy.

Tightening up our finances to prepare for whatever may happen seemed to be the prudent thing to do. The extra house was definitely a luxury, but I refused to give it up. I compromised by agreeing to rent it out during the winters to a nice retired couple from up north.

The renters moved into the lake house every fall in October and usually went back home at the end of April. I went nearly insane during those winter months, but the rental income paid its mortgage, and provided enough money to fund many of my renovation projects during the rest of the year.

I had hoped it was a quick fix to a short-term problem, but after a couple of years the economy still showed no signs of improving.

Fortunately, the renters were very nice people, and they didn't mind me dropping in now and then. It had become my safe place, and I still needed it.

THE EVENT

CHAPTER TWENTY-NINE

Recession

At the start of 2008, the Great Recession was gathering steam. Telecom markets were hemorrhaging, and Nortel was fighting for its life, along with other giants like Nokia and Motorola. But it was Nortel's name that had become almost synonymous with sweeping layoffs that had loyal employees nervous, and working longer hours to cover for the comrades already cut loose from that sinking ship. Rod and I each knew people or their spouses who had been unemployed for months, if not years, and still couldn't find work. The news was grim. But bad news from Nortel had begun long before the Great Recession.

Nortel's particular death spiral began shortly after the Y2K (Year 2000) scare when their stock price peaked at a delicious $124.50 per share and the company boasted 90,000 employees worldwide. Black October, 2000, was the first of the many major tumbles Nortel would make, its stock eventually worth just 67 cents per share two years later in October 2002. A series of alleged accounting errors, revolving door CEOs, fraud charges, and downsizing their workforce by huge numbers marked the following years. The workforce had been whittled to about 32,000 worldwide by March 2008, with more devastating news on the horizon.

The evening of Monday, March 3, 2008, Rod told me he had just received his 20-year performance review at Nortel. He reported it was an excellent review; he had been given a healthy raise in pay, and a gift of a rolling suitcase as a twenty-year anniversary gift. He was very pleased with himself. We celebrated with dinner at our favorite Mexican food restaurant, Tino's.

The following week he quietly admitted to me he'd been laid off. That was all he said at first and I thought it odd that he would be included in a lay off in the wake of such a good review. I prodded for more detail.

"When did that happen?"

"Tuesday morning. Last week," he replied.

"The day after your review?"

"Yes," he stated flatly.

"And, and…they just…What?"

His eyes fluttered with irritation at my inquiry as they had so many times before. "They called me at home, Tuesday morning, and said I needed to come in before 9 am."

"Then what? Why before 9 am?"

He crossed his arms over his chest and sucked in a deep breath, "Because they didn't want the other employees to see me packing up my desk." He hesitated for a moment and, impatient with me, chose to look at the corner of the ceiling, as if there was something up there. I knew better than to follow his gaze, there was nothing there. Long ago I had realized that was an avoidance tactic. I just had to wait him out.

Finally, realizing I wasn't going to let it go, he said, "I went to Human Resources, they gave me that suitcase and told me to pack up my shit and get out."

I don't know if anyone in the Human Resources Department was quite that brutal; more likely Rod was paraphrasing, but that's how it must have seemed to him because that's how he explained what happened. Rod tried to act unaffected, but I could see he was suffering.

"I am so sorry." I tried to hug him, but he stood without responding. My hands dropped to his waist as I stood in front of him, waiting for him to look at me. He refused, and kept staring off into the corner.

"You know, we're going to be fine," I said, "We've known this would likely happen, and our finances are in excellent shape. Everything's going to work out."

"How do you figure *that*?" He brought his eyes down to finally look at me, and the look he gave me was pure contempt.

I ignored his hateful look and continued, "Well, we're both healthy, no kids at home, we have two homes, and a good amount of savings. We are in a way better situation to weather this than a lot of people. We should be happy about that."

I thought I was being supportive and encouraging, but that was another place Rod and I had always differed.

He snorted and walked away. I watched him climb the stairs and go into his office.

I get that it's hard for a man to lose his job, and if it happened the way Rod told it, it definitely would have been devastating. I understand that men, in particular, tie up a lot of their self-worth in their work.

I get all that, but c'mon, I thought to myself, *it's not like somebody died.* I guess that was the nurse in me; everything bad is judged against if somebody died. *Death is the only thing that's final,* I was thinking.

Losing a job? A job you've worked at for twenty years? That's sort of a death, and being booted out in the way he described would be comparable to a divorce, I supposed. He had earned the right to be upset, and even a depression of some sort would be a reasonable expectation. But eventually people expect you to dust yourself off and get on with life.

Rod's mood picked up marginally over the next few days as he worked on his resume. As part of his severance package Nortel had included three months of outplacement career services that was supposed to help the freshly severed employees with resume writing, job searches, and they even dangled possible job placement back at Nortel. So, energized, Rod eagerly attended those first few days.

When I noticed he had not gotten out of bed a couple of mornings in a row to go to the group meetings, I asked why. Rod said he had done his resume but they kept telling him it needed more work, but he didn't know what else to do with it. He didn't ask me to look at it, but I found a copy on his desk and read it. More accurately, I *tried* to read it. It was four pages of tightly typed paragraphs, listing every type of telephonic project he had worked on at Nortel over the past 20 years all in excruciatingly technical detail. It was no wonder they kept telling him to work on it. I waited a couple more days, then asked how his resume was coming along.

He ignored me. I waited. There was a prescribed segment of time I had learned to wait before asking the same question again. Or, more accurately, before I added more conversation to the same subject I had just raised. If I waded in too fast, he would blow up. He was like Bob in that sense. When the time was right, I powered ahead.

"I'm just thinking that since I've had to dust off my resume several times over the last twenty years, and you haven't had to, maybe I can help you streamline yours a little bit," I offered.

He continued ignoring me. As was usual for Rod, he acted as if I didn't exist.

"Or, maybe not." I said to myself, then went on about what I was doing.

Rod spent the next couple of weeks sending out his resume. The one he had written. The one the recruiters had told him needed work. The one that I felt fairly certain no one except another telephonic communication company would understand. And he sent it to every large company in the Dallas area: Frito-Lay, American Airlines, Kimberly Clark, JC Penny, all of them. He must have sent out fifty or more online resumes and job applications. That seemed ambitious on the surface, but the downside to blasting yourself out over the internet en mass is that he almost immediately got back fifty some odd letters of rejection.

It was clear to me Rod was on the edge of depression, or had already begun the descent. A few days later I broached the subject and got a response I hadn't expected.

"I've already seen Dr. Lowe. I'm taking medication," Rod announced.

"Really? Well, that's great, really good, it's best to be proactive with that sort of thing." I knew I was babbling, "I mean a lot of people don't, and even if you aren't feeling badly depressed it can sneak up on you, so good for you getting ahead of it. Which drug did he put you on?" But Rod had spoken all the words he was going to allow the conversation, and had gone back to ignoring me.

Whatever, I thought, *as long as he's being treated*.

It was a full three days later that Rod dropped his resume in front of me and said, "I don't see how you think you can do better than this, but go ahead and try."

Revamping his resume was easy. I had already thought about it and had decided simplicity was the way to go. He had worked at the same company for twenty years, and at his previous employment for four years, so there really only needed to be those two entries. I cleaned up the job descriptions into two tidy paragraphs written in plain English, drawing on his basic marketing and business experiences, which went well with his bachelor's degree in marketing, added a photo at the top, and voila, a one-page resume that could be sent anywhere. I left it on his desk upstairs.

I didn't have to wait long to get a reaction.

"Oh. Oh, so you want to minimize what I've done for twenty-five years into a resume that couldn't get me a job selling hamburgers?" he yelled from his office, his voice dripping with hostility. "Sure, THANKS KATH-EEE. THANKS A LOT," and he threw the single paper from upstairs letting it float down to me. "Are you fucking embarrassed of me? Is THAT it? Don't do me any more favors, you fucking bitch..." as he slammed his office door.

Seemed he didn't like it.

It occurred to me his anti-depressants weren't working as well as mine had, and I again wondered what he had been taking.

Occasionally at night I checked Rod's calendar to see what he was doing. It showed monthly appointments with Dr. Lowe, which was a comfort. I didn't see the need to question him further about his medications; he was apparently getting regular follow ups. He was also seeing his dentist, having some old caps replaced, he continued running on the treadmill every day, meticulously tracked his weight, and was generally taking care of himself like he always had, so by the look of things, he had a handle on his depression. Maybe this really *was* the best he could be, under the circumstances.

My Monday-through-Friday job was with a start-up company called iVital. We provided high-end bariatric surgery services. I was working sales as well as being the nurse doing follow-up care until we had more business. In addition to iVital, and doing evening and weekend seminars, I also worked a few weekend night shifts at the hospital. There wasn't anything I could do to help Rod, and I was happy to stay at the lake house and out of his way as much as possible. Weeks passed and nothing changed.

At the end of May, two months after he'd been laid off, we went to Iowa to join his family in celebrating his father's 80th birthday. During the party, Rod confided to his younger brother Steve, that he had been laid off from Nortel. Steve thought it had just happened, and Rod made no attempt to correct his assumption.

Back at home, Rod was scheduled for a couple of interviews. One was for a position at Nortel, at a pay grade lower than his former position. He seemed really confident about going back to Nortel, and seemed to think this was in the bag. It wasn't. And neither was another position he felt sure of, one where the interviewer was a woman who lived on the same street as us, a woman who had invited the entire neighborhood to her home for Christmas parties every year. He was rejected for that position as well.

Rod began looking at alternative types of work. He seemed stymied at times, unable to decide what to apply for. I encouraged him to join a club or two. The Lions Club or Kiwanis Club, I suggested. I thought it would help him to just get out of the house, and being around other men with contacts couldn't hurt either. But Rod didn't do that. He kept sending out on-line resumes and applications.

Rod applied for and started receiving unemployment benefits, and calculated how long he could receive the assistance. At that time in the US, with so many people out of work, those benefits were being extended over and over again, so the end date kept moving. The other part of his severance package continued his regular full pay until the end of October, 2008, and the renters were moving into the lake house on October 31st, so financially we were still in good shape.

Rod's brother Steve, came to Dallas for a business meeting in September, four months after seeing him in Iowa. Steve was only in town for a short time, and the two met for dinner at Tino's. When Steve asked Rod how the job hunt was going Rod simply stated, "It's taking longer than I thought it would."

At his monthly doctor's appointment on September 10, 2008, Rod complained of not being able to sleep. Dr. Lowe issued a prescription for Ambien, a popular sleep aid that was widely advertised on television. "Ask your doctor if Ambien is right for you," the ad encouraged its viewers. So Rod did.

Ambien, or Zolpidem Tartrate, is a hypnotic, and comes with a long and varied list of possible side effects. It is generally believed that someone under the effects of a hypnotic won't do anything they didn't already have the impulse for.

Rod took it for 28 days.

CHAPTER THIRTY

The Voice

October 7, 2008 was a Tuesday. Sales had cooled at iVital because of the depressed economy, so I had been making cold calls and following up with existing patients. The day had been uneventful and I lingered in the office after five o'clock. I always enjoyed the quiet time after the phones were switched off, and I wasn't in any hurry to get home. One of the owners was still working when I finally got up to leave and we talked for a few minutes. He asked why I hadn't left yet, and I said that home was sort of depressing.

"Rod just sits on the couch and stares at the news channel cranking out one horrendous story after another about the economy," I explained. "It's so sad."

When I got home that's exactly what Rod was doing. I changed clothes and when I came back downstairs, the television was off. Rod had poured two glasses of wine and held one out to me.

"Well thank you," I told him. "That's really sweet of you."

We settled on the couch together and turned the television back on. At seven o'clock, *Dancing with the Stars* came on, and we both commented on how well the big football player danced. He looked like he would be awkward, at the least, but he was a very smooth dancer and really seemed to enjoy himself. We both agreed that he might win the competition.

It was odd for Rod to talk so much; I noticed and enjoyed the change. At eight o'clock we switched over to watch the second presidential debate between John McCain and Barack Obama. The first five questions were all related to the failing economy, and with each one I felt increasingly uncomfortable, knowing it weighed so heavily on Rod's mind. I wished he could just get away from all the bad news for a while. We decided the debate was boring. It was a little after nine in the evening when I got up to go to bed, and was surprised when Rod turned off the TV and followed me.

But he stopped at the bottom of the stairs and seemed to be deep in thought, or upset, so I put my arms around his neck and whispered, "Everything's going to be all right."

As usual, he didn't hug me back. But in a quiet voice he said, "*You* think everything's going to be all right–but it's not."

I asked what he meant by that, but he wouldn't answer, instead he walked past me and slowly up the stairs to our bedroom. I wondered if he had lost some of our savings in a bad investment, or if this was his depression talking. I made a mental note to check our bank account balances from work in the morning.

In bed, he leaned over to kiss me and in the dark we bumped heads. We both laughed and he quoted the commercial saying, "I could've had a V8." He seemed to have flipped to an uncharacteristically good mood. Then he tickled my nose and told me, "I love you." I said I loved him too.

I fell asleep immediately and, quite unusually for me, I slept all night.

When I woke the room felt oddly cold. Turning over, I looked at the bedside clock. It was 6:28 am. As my eyes adjusted to the dark I could see Rod sitting cross-legged on the bed, facing me. He was slowly rocking side to side. As my sleep fogged brain began to clear, I could hear him mumbling to himself but I was unable to make out the words.

"What are you doing?" I asked. I propped myself on my elbows and saw that he was holding something in his hands. "Rod, why are you awake? It's only 6:30," I asked again.

"I'm meditating," he responded quietly. I stifled a laugh. To my knowledge, Rod had never meditated in his entire life. The thought of him turning into a yogi overnight was a heck of a stretch. "I haven't slept all night," he added.

That seemed odd, since I'd slept so soundly. I asked him why, and what was on his mind, but he said nothing. I reached up and pulled him down onto the bed in front of me. His shoulder and arm felt cold and his muscles were tense to my touch. I lay behind him, something he typically didn't like, but this time he didn't move away. I tried to warm him by rubbing his right arm. I quickly fell back to sleep.

I awoke again at 7:25 am, an hour later, even though the alarm wasn't set to go off until seven-thirty. Rod was sitting cross legged again and seemed to be chanting. I strained to make out the words this time, but his voice was low and the words sounded slurred. Then I heard him say, "...but you would find someone else."

"What did you say?" I sat bolt upright. I could see Rod still held something in his hands. With more morning light filtering into the room I could now see it was a paperweight. It was a perfectly round, polished, solid marble sphere with a single flat spot. It had previously been on a shelf next to his desk in the adjoining room. It weighed about five pounds.

Rod stopped rocking and chanting and sat perfectly still. I asked again what was going on, if he was okay, but he didn't answer. He was back to not speaking.

Frustrated with his lack of response I said, "Well, I guess I'll go take a shower," and got out of bed.

Since the layoff, Rod's routine had changed dramatically, and often he got out of bed when my alarm went off. He had assumed the responsibility of taking the dogs downstairs to let them out into our backyard while I took my shower and got dressed. This morning, he hopped out of bed when I did, and got as far as the top of the stairs, then stood looking down onto the tile surface below. Very gently, without looking at me, he waved me toward him with his right hand.

"Come here," he said in a crystal clear voice, "Come here and talk to me." He was holding the paperweight in his left hand, down at his side, seemingly trying to hide it behind his leg.

I didn't move.

"Please come here, I want to talk to you," he said again in a very normal voice, then turned his head and looked at me with his eyes lowered.

I almost did. But as I looked at him standing there, at the top of the stairs, holding that solid marble paperweight, I knew something was wrong.

"No, I'm going to go take a shower and get dressed, we'll talk then. Okay?" I ducked into the bathroom and as quietly as I could, I locked the door. I had never locked that door before.

What's going on? What the hell is he doing with that marble ball? What should I do? I stood looking at myself in the mirror and thought, *Kathi, you're a nurse, assess him like you would any patient.*

I could call the police but what could I say, that my husband was acting weird and carrying a marble ball? The first question they'd ask would be, "Has he hurt you, or threatened to hurt you?" and I would have to answer no. Then they would ask, "Has he threatened to hurt himself or anyone else?" and my answer again would be no. It occurred to me that it was not against the law to carry a paperweight and act strange, and reporting it wouldn't get me a helpful response.

I tried to think of anyone else I could call, but there was no one; no close friend, no co-worker, no priest, and no doctor at that hour. I decided that since he had gotten out of bed his voice at least seemed to be stronger, maybe he had been disoriented from not sleeping, and now with the sun fully up things would look clearer to him and he would be okay. I decided there was nothing else I could do but get ready for work and proceed as if he were fine.

I showered and dressed in black slacks and a black tank top. I chose a print blouse to put on when I was ready to go. I had dried my hair and was applying my blush and lip gloss when I heard a knock on the door. He didn't speak, it was just a light tapping on the door.

"I'll be out in a couple of minutes," I called to him. But I hesitated. I stood looking at myself in the mirror for the second time that morning, and said a quick prayer that Rod would be clear headed now and everything would be fine.

I unlocked the door and slowly opened it. There was no sound in the house and I wondered if I was alone. The sun was streaming in through the downstairs front windows. I looked for him at the top of the stairs but Rod wasn't there.

I opened the door a bit further to see if he had gone back to bed as he sometimes did. But the bed was empty and unmade.

I saw a slight movement out of the corner of my left eye that made me look further into the room when abruptly, Rod stepped out from behind the bathroom door into full view. He stood tall with his arms extended fully over his head, the paperweight gripped in both hands. His eyes were opened wide and wild, showing more white than iris, his mouth was open, and his teeth were clenched tightly together.

"No," I instinctively whispered as I reached out to place my right hand on his chest. He stood trembling for a breath of a second, then brought the marble rock down squarely on the top of my skull with a crushing force.

I sensed my body crumple. My legs became useless. I saw the room as if through shattered glass, familiar things at odd angles and in the wrong directions. I could hear someone scream, far off at first, then closer until I realized it was me. I fell sideways and backward, my movements thick and uncontrolled. I struggled to stay upright but my legs didn't respond properly. I could feel the pressure of Rod's weight against me, falling against me, pushing me down as my legs thrashed out of control.

Then the fog cleared and I was on the floor looking up, with him straddling my chest. He held my right shoulder with his left hand and raised his right hand holding the marble rock, arced his arm high behind his head and brought it down hard and fast, until it connected with the left side of my head. My arms responded by flying upward to cover my face and I heard screaming again.

After that second crushing blow, I had an explosion of thoughts–not a stream, but a sudden flood of information that came to me all at once–in a splinter of an instant. I was immediately aware of some simple truths, but in a clear and chronological order. I don't know how to explain this, they might have been my own memories, or possibly a spiritual connection. Whatever it was, I was delivered a group of thoughts, the clarity of which was truly amazing.

Stop screaming–you're wasting oxygen and energy. Besides, no one can hear you.

*He's going to kill you. This isn't a beating, it isn't a probability; he **IS** going to kill you.*

You need to fight back. You aren't a little kid anymore.

*Do **NOT** die like a coward; the only thing you can do now is to leave evidence that you tried. You owe that to yourself, to your children, your granddaughters, your sisters, your nieces, **ALL** the people in your life need to know you did **NOT** die hiding in a corner like a coward.*

And finally an echo of Horse's proud voice on the day Sam died "***We would expect nothing less.***"

I didn't question the validity of these thoughts. The knowledge didn't scare me. They were undeniable facts.

But as I looked at Rod, I paused. I didn't want to hurt him. This was a man I cared about. I searched his face and tried to make eye contact. Then he brought the rock down on my head a third time, and my decision was made.

"*Think. What can you do?*" The voice asked.

I drew in as deep a breath as I could with him sitting on my chest, and at the same time, I grabbed his right wrist with my left hand and locked my elbow with my arm straight. He was far stronger than me, and was able to overpower my straightened arm and continue pounding the marble rock into my skull, but the blows lacked their previous impact, and with each hit I consciously turned my face away to minimize the damage.

Then I dug the two forefingers of my right hand deep into his eye sockets, and locked my thumb under his chin. Surprised, he jerked back and away from my hand and stopped hitting me, but I hung on, my hand latched to his face, and I saw a tiny space had opened between our bodies. I pulled my knees up and wriggled until my feet were flat on his chest, then I sucked in another deep breath and kicked out as hard as I could.

He was thrown off me and fell backward, with his mid-back, head and shoulders over the bathtub edge, and he'd lost his hold on the paperweight. It fell from his right hand and hit the bathroom carpet leaving a ring of blood where it landed. As I scrambled to reach it, Rod struggled to sit upright, and he raced to get to the rock before I did. I could see his hand was fractionally closer to it than mine.

"*Run,*" said the voice in my head.

I staggered to my knees, then feet, and ran in an ungainly motion, almost getting through the bathroom door before I felt Rod's hand on the back of my head, grabbing chunks of my hair. I wrenched free, and got into the bedroom but realized he was with me and blocked the exit door to the stairs.

"*What's in this room,*" the voice demanded, "*What can you use?*"

I mentally scanned the room and recalled a fairly heavy garden statue that sat next to a standing mirror behind the bathroom door. I reached down and felt the edge of the piece with my fingertips, then wrapped my hand around the main body of it.

"*Swing it like a baseball bat,*" the voice said, "*Don't hold back, put everything you've got into it.*"

I swung that statue with every bit of strength I had, and felt the centrifugal force take hold as I turned toward him. The statue hit Rod full in his face and disintegrated into a million pieces on impact. He didn't flinch at the assault; it seemed he didn't even feel pain. He grabbed one of the larger chunks of the statue as it fell and attacked me again, beating my face and head as I retreated into the bathroom. There was little room between us but I was able to close the door before he got in – so I thought. My eyes were on the lock mechanism in the doorknob, and I couldn't understand why the door wouldn't quite close. I looked up and saw the obstruction. The outstretched fingers of Rod's right hand were wrapped tightly around the edge of the door. I jerked frantically on the door knob, desperate to cut off his fingers and pull it shut.

Rod worked the door open just enough to get his left hand holding the piece of broken statue through, then his arm was inside, and he let go of the door with his right hand. He raked at me wildly with the broken piece as I fought to hold the door shut. Again, being far stronger than me, he grasped the door with his right hand and ripped it open, charged in and hit me hard, knocking me to the floor again. As I fell, he collected the paperweight he had dropped by the bathtub, and I found myself back in the same position as before, on my back trying to lock my elbow while he continued to strike me with the marble rock. Only this time he held my right arm down and away from his face.

"*What else can you do?*" the voice asked. I frantically tried to think of what I might be able to use, if there was anything within my reach, but there was nothing. After a few more hits, I realized that my left arm was all but useless, nearly limp, and I could no longer lock my elbow between the blows.

Strength flowed out of me like water from a hose.

"*You're dying,*" the voice said calmly. Then, "*what else can you do?*"

My mind was blank as the dull thuds pounded over and over against my head. I was no longer able to turn my face away. I accepted I was about to die.

Very serenely the voice then said, "*He wants you dead. Be dead.*" As if the angel who had been coaching from my shoulder had shrugged, unable to think of anything more to do, finally gave me permission to die.

I obeyed. I had no fight left. My body went completely limp.

I spoke, or tried to speak, "You can stop now; I'm dead."

Maybe it was nothing more than garbled sound, but I did speak those words aloud, and Rod seemed to have heard me. I briefly worried he would see me breathing, when the reality struck that I was not, in fact, breathing. I wasn't deliberately holding my breath, I simply wasn't breathing and not one hair on me was moving. I was totally unconcerned by that fact.

Rod sat back on his knees and watched me. He was breathing quite heavily.

I could see him, but my eyes were fixed, unable to move. I wondered if I had already died.

I saw Rod slowly raise the paperweight high above his head again and hold it there. He waited, just a second or two, while he studied me. I wondered what he was thinking.

"*Don't move, don't move, don't move,*" the voice chanted. I didn't. I couldn't.

Then, having decided, Rod brought the sphere down on my left ear and jaw in one final pounding blow.

On impact I was aware of my entire upper body lifting off the floor then dropping back down in a heap, my jaw displaced at an odd angle.

Rod sat back on his knees looking at me again, his face contorted in an ugly sneer.

Satisfied I was dead, he slowly got to his feet, dropped the marble ball at my side, and staggered to the door, where he stopped and steadied himself, holding onto the door jamb with his right hand as he caught his breath. He had his back to me finally, and it crossed my mind that if I was still alive, I badly needed to get air into my lungs.

I needed to breathe. But nothing happened.

I had a sense of being on a precipice. I felt quite comfortable being dead. Knowing my body lay in a heap didn't concern me. I didn't feel pain, or fear; I felt nothing. I sensed myself moving closer toward that edge, painlessly drifting like vapor into the space beyond, with nothing impeding my descent. At that moment I had absolutely no thought about anyone or anything. I was at total peace.

"*Breathe,*" the voice said.

I didn't. Doing nothing was so simple; so perfect.

I was easing closer to the edge, and could see an endless chasm below, when the voice said more urgently, "*You need to breathe. BREATHE NOW.*"

The command startled me. With enormous effort, I felt my chest rise as I drew in a short gasp. A fraction of a breath. But it was enough. Enough to bring me back to the present, and I realized Rod was still standing with his back to me at the bathroom door.

"*You've got one chance to get him out of here. Take a big breath and do it,*" the voice ordered.

I drew in a second breath, deeper into my lungs, and sat up.

The bloodied marble ball lay beside me. I picked it up and struggled to my feet. Fearing he would hear me or sense I was moving, I knew I had to act quickly. But my body wasn't responding well, and quickly wasn't happening. I launched my whole body at him as hard as I could and planted the paperweight squarely in the center of his back. Incredibly, he flew forward, with much more force than I'd delivered, out through the bathroom door, landing on his hands and knees, his face to the carpeted floor. The paperweight fell into the bedroom and landed beside him.

I saw my right hand as the marble ball made contact with his back, and in slow motion I watched my wrist and arm flop downward. The impact from my body felt like no more than a gentle shove. It was a pathetically weak effort, but somehow, it had worked.

My hands began shaking as I grabbed the bathroom door, pulled it shut, and fumbling with fingers slick with blood, I miraculously turned the lock. There was no sound from the other side of the door. I turned around and looked back into the bathroom.

There was blood everywhere. Blood smeared on the walls, a huge pool of it where my head had been, blood trails from the door, and splatter everywhere.

"*Don't look at the mirror,*" the voice instructed. I didn't.

On rubbery legs, I held onto the walls and counter until I reached the toilet room where there was a wall telephone. Once inside I pulled the door shut and let my body slide down the wall onto the floor. There was still no noise from beyond the bathroom.

There was no lock on that toilet room door, and it opened outward. Rod had to know I was alive now, and he could easily open the bathroom door; it was one of those locks that you can pick with a hairpin. If he got back inside the bathroom, I would be totally defenseless as I couldn't jam this door closed, so I wrapped my left hand around the doorknob and pulled on it, holding it shut.

With my right hand I got the receiver and dialed 911. I heard a busy signal.

I hoped for guidance, but the voice no longer spoke to me.

I pressed the switch hook disconnecting the call, and tried to think what else I could do. There was only one window in that second story bathroom, and it was covered with double-paned steel reinforced glass. I realized the phone was my only hope.

Maybe Rod had cut the line. If he had gone into the kitchen he could see the light on the main phone that would tell him it was in use. Releasing the switch hook, I heard a dial tone, and with my right thumb I again punched in the numbers 911.

"Plano Police Department, what is your emergency--"

"He's killing me," I said quietly.

"He's KILLING you?" the operator responded.

"Yes, YES, he's killing me," I pleaded. I couldn't think of any other way to describe what had happened.

I knew that even though I hadn't yet lost consciousness I could still be dying. Subdural hematomas, fractured skull, bleeding in or around the brain, stroke, brain swelling, blood clots, any number of complications can come from a traumatic head injury, and I had taken several extremely hard hits. I rushed to give the 911 operator as much information as I could, before the inevitable blackness set in and I died. I was sure that would happen. Maybe in the next few minutes, or maybe not for a few hours. But it would happen, I was certain of it.

I gave my full address, named Rod as my assailant, and briefly described what had occurred. I wanted to give a medical report on myself but my brain wasn't working well and I could only repeat that I had multiple head injuries and needed help. I tried to think of more but couldn't.

The 911 Operator told me, "Don't hang up. Stay on the line with me."

I begged her to hurry. I prayed to God that they would hurry.

I began to assess myself. I looked at my hands and arms and saw they were black, not dusky but totally black. Was that blood? Certainly some of it was, but they seemed universally black, worse than just cyanotic. How was that possible? Even more disturbing were my fingernails–they were solid white, strangely raised and pulled away from their nail beds. I had never seen that before. Then I noticed my hair. It had been shoulder length but now long bloody chunks of hair hung halfway down my left upper arm, and I understood that the side of my scalp was partly detached.

I heard Rod yell. I didn't hear words, only yelling, like an animal. It sounded like he was downstairs.

The 911 operator kept assuring me that officers were on their way. Again I begged them to hurry.

Finally, she told me they were at my location, and I could hear banging on the front door and shouting. I told the operator they would have to break down the door.

But Rod apparently unlocked and opened the front door for them, and I could hear several voices inside the house yelling. Lots of yelling.

Then I heard a sound that absolutely terrified me and a scream rose from me that I could neither stop nor control.

Someone fired a gun.

"Does your husband have a gun?" the operator asked, over and over. I was out of my head, in full panic. Had Rod shot at me through the ceiling? Had the police fired a warning shot? Who had the gun? I was sure more bullets were coming.

Rod screamed my name, one pleading scream, "KAATH-EE", then everything downstairs went quiet.

The yelling stopped, but I heard footsteps on the stairs, then in the bedroom at the bathroom door.

"Don't open that door," the operator yelled at me. "DO NOT OPEN THAT DOOR!" she yelled.

I didn't. I strained even harder to hold the door shut, fighting the panic that swept over me in great waves.

"DON'T OPEN THAT DOOR UNTIL YOU KNOW WHO IT IS," she yelled and every time she said it I tightened my grip on the door knob.

I heard voices, lots of voices, then a single knock. A garbled, helpless sound that only injured animals make escaped my throat.

I heard a man's strong voice, "We're the police, Kathi, are you in here?"

I slowly pried my fingers loose and let my arm drop to my side, and let him open the door.

Sitting on the floor of that tiny space, in a pool of blood, fear made me cower against the wall when their hands reached in to help me.

CHAPTER THIRTY-ONE

Investigation

In the bright light of day, the sky and the grass were almost painful to look at, their colors were so vivid. There were fluffy white clouds in a very blue sky, and the temperature was warm with a cool breeze.

How could such a horrible thing happen on a beautiful day like this?

As they rolled the gurney across the street toward the ambulance, a policeman threw himself across me, and yelled, "Don't let those kids see."

I was aware of many police officers, ambulances, and people lining the sidewalks. I was vaguely aware of the whump, whump sound of helicopter blades above me.

I overheard the Emergency Medical Techs (EMTs) discussing where they should take me. The bus carrying Rod had just left for the Medical Center of Plano about five miles away. They spoke about some rule that in domestic violence cases, they weren't supposed to take both parties to the same hospital. I didn't care where they took me, I didn't care which hospital I went to; and I was reminded of a fast ride in a red corvette from my ancient past.

I was loaded into the waiting ambulance where I gave my contact information. My body began to shake.

The EMTs, it seemed, received approval to take us both to the Medical Center of Plano. I had worked at that hospital as a telemetry tech during nursing school, then as a Registered Nurse in the Intensive Care Unit after graduating. I knew many of the nurses who worked there, and had been friends with the Vice President of Nursing while I was in school. I was acquainted with the ER Nurse Manager, Amy, though I didn't know her well. They were all excellent nurses, and I couldn't think of a better hospital for care. I wasn't concerned about Rod being at the same hospital. Certainly he'd be in handcuffs, and there would be loads of people around.

I was aware of the muted siren and the bus moving, and I drifted off to confusing memories, as dreams often are.

On arrival in the ER, a nurse cut off my clothes. I was initially perturbed when she took out her bandage scissors and started at my ankle, the blades hacking my pants off. Those were really nice pants, and I thought if I had been given a minute I could have gotten them off without damage, but she was practiced with her scissors and was well into the butchery before I could say anything. As I watched the destruction, I noticed the blood on them. I kept quiet. Once the pants were ruined, it was nothing to let her cut off my tank top and bra, then I watched as she deposited the whole messy blob into a plastic go-home bag that I would never see again. I was helped into a standard-issue hospital gown.

So this is what it is like to be a patient, I thought. It was a strange place to be. Everyone had a job to do and they went about it fast and efficiently. I knew the drill, but I couldn't get a handle on my anxiety. If everything and everybody would just slow down and give me some time. Everything was going so fast. My head felt disconnected.

I heard an endless stream of people walk by. Some pulled back the curtain and looked in, then moved on. Policemen stopped and looked in at me, but didn't speak. Maybe they were looking for someone else. The Police chaplain came in and introduced himself, and just as quickly, he stepped out again. Then a detective entered and introduced himself.

He took a position on the left side of my gurney, got out a small tablet and pen, and asked if I could answer a few questions.

"Yes," I said.

"So, you two just woke up and started fighting, is that it?"

"No," I answered slowly. "There was no fight."

He dropped his hands by his side, his shoulders slumped, and he stared at me with big, unbelieving eyes.

I instantly realized my mistake.

"No. Um, I mean there was no argument. Obviously, there was a fight."

He raised his pen to the tablet again. "Did you lose consciousness?"

"No," I said quietly, "I remember everything. I... I can tell you everything that happened." Then I hesitated, and more to myself than to the detective I added, "What I can't tell you is why."

I started from when Rod was laid off, the suitcase, the job search, the depression, the night before, and then every detail from that morning.

"Did he say anything?" the detective asked.

"No, the last time he spoke was when he wanted to talk to me at the top of the stairs," I said. "He never said another word after that."

Then he was done. He closed his notebook and didn't ask anything else.

Just outside my curtain I overheard the detective speak to someone, who I suspected was another police officer, and I heard the words "… murder-suicide..."

A different man's voice said, "There was another one this morning in California. Unemployed father shot and killed his wife and four kids, even the family dog. This economy… we're going to be seeing a lot more of these."

Then I was alone again on the gurney until a doctor came to stitch up my head and foot. I had a half-moon gash on the arch of my right foot, but I had no idea when or how that happened. Some of the wounds on my head were sort of smashed, and the doctor said he was having difficulty deciding how to pull everything back together.

He said he didn't want to cut my hair and explained, "The trauma alone is bad enough, and we don't like to add to it by chopping the patient's hair off if we can avoid it."

I told him I'd rather he cut whatever hair he needed to in order to see what he was doing, and he did. It took some time but when he was done, he counted thirteen sutured lacerations on my head, which required over 250 stitches and staples to close, as well as a few smaller places that remained open.

When he was finished, I asked for a mirror. My hair was in ragged tufts, my face unevenly swollen, and my left ear stuck out at a 90-degree angle like the blinker on a truck. I couldn't move my left arm and hand, and my lower jaw wasn't behaving like it should.

I searched for my own face as I stared at the reflection.

A new doctor came in and told me that after looking at the results of my CT scan, amazing as it seemed, there was nothing critically wrong with me. He made the comment "I don't understand how you weren't more seriously injured."

I didn't either. *I am alive. I. Am. Alive. And there wasn't anything critically wrong. Had I imagined everything? Had I made a mistake? He did try to kill me, I was sure of that. How could there not be anything critically wrong with me? What about when I wasn't breathing? What had caused that?*

I laid my head back onto the pillow and tried to let my mind go blank and just concentrate on breathing. I closed my eyes. I needed to slow things down. Breathe in, breathe out, let the tension escape.

I heard the sound of the curtain being pulled back again. A man in green surgical scrubs walked to the right of my bed. He introduced himself and said, "I'm the surgeon who has been taking care of your husband."

"Oh, thank you," I said as I took his hand, then asked, "How is he?" I pictured Rod in police custody, in handcuffs, maybe with a few scrapes and scratches from being arrested.

"Well," the doctor began, pointing to his sternum, "the bullet entered his chest here..."

"Wait, wait," I interrupted him, and tried to raise myself up. "The BULLET?" I asked, "He was SHOT?"

The surgeon searched my face, his own eyes clouded, and asked, "You didn't know he was shot?"

"No...no," I stammered. The events replayed in my brain as I tried to put this together with what I already knew. "I knew there was a gunshot. But I didn't...I didn't know HE was shot..."

The surgeon sighed then continued with the information he had come to deliver.

"As I said, the bullet entered his chest here," he again pointed to his mid sternal area, "and it travelled behind his liver and tore up some big blood vessels. He bled internally. Once he was in the ER he received multiple transfusions. We prepped him for the operating room, but as he was transferred onto the table he stopped breathing. Mrs. Jensen, we tried to revive him but he died."

As a nurse, I had heard this news delivered to families countless times. I had never been on the receiving side of the conversation. It was beyond devastating to hear, beyond comprehension to accept. I couldn't imagine Rod dead. It wasn't possible.

This entire day everything had been wrong. My world was upside down, the earth had shifted below me—it had been knocked off its axis and was spinning out of control.

Just STOP! Everything needed to stop. I became aware of two of me, the Kathi I knew who had almost been bludgeoned to death, and the Kathi who was now in a hospital bed faced with facts she never imagined. I was fractured, each one of me traveling on her own trajectory in opposite directions. I wondered if the two Kathis would ever converge and be whole again.

LeAndra pulled the curtain aside, followed by my daughter. They each took one of my hands as if to steady me as I fell though the abyss. I couldn't breathe. A nurse was called. She told me I was hyperventilating and needed to calm down. I couldn't, now that I desperately wanted to, I couldn't breathe. I began to panic. I clawed at the hands holding me, at the tubes, at whatever I could reach. The nurse injected a sedative into my IV.

I woke in a private room, a suite that is usually reserved for VIPs. It was deluxe accommodations for a hospital, and was attached to an anteroom, where families could gather and not spill into the hall. It was a luxury I could never have anticipated, but one I was grateful for.

The room itself was darkened and quiet, which was good, as noise made my head hurt. I lay still and slowly recalled the recent events. Rod was dead. I was fine. An incredibly odd outcome to how the day had started. I had been so sure it would be just the opposite.

Debbie immediately flew in from Louisiana, as I knew she would, and I so appreciated seeing her.

My brothers-in-law Steve and Roger and their wives Diane and Sue arrived from Iowa.

Steve charged into my room, straight up to my face, and half-shouted, "You have to tell me what happened, you have to tell me everything that happened, because I just don't understand."

"I will," I told him quietly, "I'll tell you everything, but I can't tell you *why*. I don't *know* why."

Steve seemed angry, an emotion I hadn't expected. Their loss didn't register with me until later, that he and Roger had just lost their brother. I hadn't absorbed the full ramifications of Rod being dead. I was still marveling that I had lived. I knew I'd missed something because Steve had always been so happy to see me, and this time was different, but I didn't understand why. It felt somewhat like swimming toward the water's surface but not quite breaking through; an understanding just beyond my reach.

I suddenly felt a sickness, a nausea that wasn't from my stomach. I struggled to stand but found my legs were less than reliable. I somehow got to the opposite wall and found a basin before heaving bile uncontrollably. It felt as if the pressure would surely split my broken head open and all of me would come spewing out. It wouldn't stop. I was almost too weak to stand, and I clutched the counter; laid over it. I could feel the bitter sickness roll from my pelvis all the way up through my throat. Finally, a nurse arrived and gave me a shot of Phenergan, an antiemetic, and within minutes I was able to return to bed, and sleep.

Each time I woke it was the same, peace at first, then the thoughts and feelings crept into my head like daylight through an open window. I felt an enormous loss of everything familiar to me. Sure, Rod was an ass, but he was the ass I'd lived with for almost twenty-one years and now he was gone. Blinked out of existence. I had trusted Rod to never hit me. I had stayed with him because I believed he wouldn't.

I had had my head smashed in and was sure I would die, now just a few hours later, not only was I alive, but Rod was dead. It was a confusing mix of feelings knowing my life had changed so dramatically in just a few hours. *I survived. Rod was dead. How is that possible?* Those three phrases kept going through my head.

Slowly, gradually, the nausea and vomiting subsided. My jaw wouldn't open more than a fraction and I tried sipping water through a straw. Food was unbearable, but I felt that carbohydrate-poor emptiness, my body telling me I needed to eat. I began breaking crumbs of bread and poking them through the tiny space between my lips as often as I could.

I was in the hospital for two nights, and during that time LeAndra's husband Curt had arranged for a crime scene cleaning company to go to my house. Curt let me know there was too much blood on the bathroom carpet; it was unsalvageable and had to be ripped out. There were also some blood stains on the bedroom carpet they had been unable to remove, but rather than take out that large piece of carpet, they cleaned it as best they could and let the stains remain.

Curt and LeAndra had found my two dogs and taken them to their house to care for them. I was lucky to have such good friends.

I soon learned more of the facts of what went on with Rod downstairs, while I had been hiding upstairs.

Rod had opened the front door holding a knife to his throat. The first police officer on the scene that day ordered him to drop it.

"I can't do it," Rod had said, then lunged at the officers, and was shot.

Rod's brothers asked why the police hadn't used a stun gun on him, rather than shooting him. But when an unbalanced person is wielding a knife, police can't risk trying to get close enough to stun him.

Rod had refused to speak to the EMTs or the nurses at the hospital. The only thing he said, after the ER manager Amy told him he would be intubated for surgery, was "DNR", a common acronym for "do not resuscitate." She told me later that many patients had said that to her over her years in the ER, but when Rod said it, she believed he really wanted to die.

Before I was released from the hospital, the chaplain came to my bedside. He asked if I had any suicidal thoughts—if there was a chance I might go home depressed and want to end my life.

"No," I said, and this time there was no hesitation. I smiled and shook my head. The one thing I was sure of was I wouldn't kill myself. "I didn't fight that hard to stay alive, just to go home and kill myself."

Beth brought a change of clothes to the hospital for me, a pair of jeans, and a tank top along with a zip up hoodie. The plan was to go to Beth's home and decide what to do from there. I had been adamant that I didn't want to go back to my house.

I thought I would go to the lake house. I knew I was being selfish and thinking only of myself, but I needed a peaceful atmosphere, and someone quiet who wouldn't ask a lot of questions, so when I left the hospital I asked Debbie to go back home. I knew her feelings were hurt, but of all my sisters it was Janie's peaceful demeanor I needed with me during my first days on my own.

As I rode in the wheelchair to the main entrance of the hospital someone asked whose car I would be riding in and I said, "The first one that drives up that I recognize, I'm getting into."

Steve pulled under the canopy first and I may have surprised him when I hopped into his back seat. His wife Diane sat in the front passenger seat. I rolled the back window down. It was sunny and crisp outside, and the air was clean and fresh. Colors were vibrant and the breeze felt like kisses on my skin. I felt like I'd been far, far away somewhere for a very long time. I filled my lungs with the fresh air and I knew I'd finally reached the surface and had broken through. I felt reborn. I couldn't help smiling. I was alive. I was very thankful to be...alive.

As Steve drove down Park Blvd, we passed the horses and cows owned by Plano's billionaire, and I could see the street my house was on. I thought how familiar and peaceful everything looked. I noticed how calm and comfortable I felt. "Alive" was the word that played over and over in my head.

"Stevie, turn here," I asked, breaking the silence, "If you don't mind. I just want to drive past the house, please."

The street and the house looked so normal. It wasn't covered in blood, nobody was out on the sidewalk, and there was no yellow crime scene tape draped around. The house didn't look evil. It was just a brick and mortar house, well maintained on a nice manicured street with a mowed lawn and the trees and shrubs I'd planted in the yard.

The three of us sat in the car looking at it for some time before Steve asked quietly, "Do you want to go inside?"

It's my home, I thought to myself. Inside, it contained my things—my clothes, my pictures, my memories. I had painted every room, hung every curtain, my DNA was in every corner of its interior. It had been two days since I'd been there, and in that time I'd died and now I was back. It was time to reclaim the rest of my life. To put the parts of me that was split apart back together.

We parked in the driveway and went inside.

#

The following day, Rod's brothers Steve and Roger came to the mortuary with me and my son Adam. I must have looked like I'd been in a car wreck with all the bruising, missing chunks of hair, and sutures all over my head. When the Funeral Director asked for Rod's cause of death, my mind went blank. I didn't know what to call it. The thing that had happened. Not murder, yet not really suicide…

Roger broke the silence and said, "He died suddenly."

The woman gave me a long, hard look while she contemplated that explanation.

"My mother died suddenly," she finally offered. "That's how I got into this business."

No one spoke as she continued to stare at me. Then she went on with the application as if "died suddenly" was a medical term that described precisely what had happened.

Some people have said it was suicide by cop, but I'm not convinced Rod intended to kill himself, but that will never be known. I've tried saying "he died suddenly" to other people but unlike the Funeral Director, most want a better explanation.

Our bank accounts were untouched. Rod had pulled his money out of Nortel stock when it first began to tumble – long before it became worthless, and we still had quite a bit of savings in his 401(K). Our personal savings were on target. Our bills were all paid up to date.

Neither of us carried life insurance policies, at least none that I was aware of. It was suggested that he may have taken one out on me and locked it into a safety deposit box somewhere. I'll never know.

It took me weeks going through every scrap of paper, every email, every message board, and all his assorted files, and I found absolutely nothing that shed any light on what had happened. I was certain he would have left some sort of note, or clue, but there was none.

I requested copies of his medical files and discovered he hadn't been prescribed an antidepressant, as he told me. Instead, he had been receiving testosterone shots monthly, for a mildly low testosterone level. And then there was Ambien.

The Food and Drug Administration lists "abnormal thoughts and behavior" as a "possible serious side effect" of Ambien. Adverse symptoms include "more outgoing or aggressive behavior than normal, confusion, agitation, hallucinations, worsening of depression, and suicidal thoughts or actions."

When Rod's autopsy came back, he had a measurable level of Zolpidem Tartrate–Ambien–in his bloodstream at the time of his death. In the weeks that followed, I wrote a four-page letter reporting it as an adverse drug effect and sent it through certified mail to Sanofi-Aventis, the company that makes Ambien. I got no response. I contacted an attorney but after a year, I was told that there was no way to prove Ambien had caused Rod to behave this way.

Actually, it may have been a perfect storm of circumstances: the lay-off, the untreated depression, and the wrong medications, but Rod certainly had culpability as well. Even under a hypnotic, I've been told repeatedly that a person will not do anything they don't already have the impulse to do.

The Medical Examiner who performed Rod's autopsy said if he had been under the influence of a hypnotic, he would certainly have been jolted awake when I hit him with the statue.

What I had to face was, regardless of the Ambien, Rod had been planning to kill me. Maybe Ambien took away that last thread of inhibition. Or maybe Rod had planned on using Ambien as his defense.

My sister Janie stayed with me for the first week after I was released from the hospital. We found rubber gloves, a roll of heavy-duty trash bags, and a shovel near Rod's Escalade truck in the garage. They hadn't been there the night of October 7th, the last time I had been in the garage. I could only hypothesize what he had planned to do with them.

There were several knives laid out on the kitchen counter and on the dining room table along with a homemade wire garrote. The garrote and the marble ball were taken by the police and are held in an evidence box.

I worried that Rod may have drugged the glass of wine he gave me the night of October 7th. It was highly unusual for me to sleep so soundly, and unheard of for me to wake up and fall back to sleep as I did that morning. In the first days after I was released from the hospital, Janie and I emptied the house of any open container that may have been tampered with.

We took down the blackout curtains in the master bedroom and replaced them with sheers that let the light in. We moved the bed from where it had been to face a different direction. We brought an 8'X5' rug from downstairs to cover the bloodstains on the carpet. I sanded off the arc scraped into the bathroom door by the statue piece and repainted it.

Afterward, my sleep pattern changed and I slept soundly through the nights.

Janie was quiet and peaceful. She helped me design and print Rod's memorial card with the words he had written in the will he had insisted we write long before we even married. Janie was the perfect person to have with me that first week.

When she left, my cousin Kim came to stay for about a week. Her gentle presence was such a comfort, and I was able to complete many of the legal issues that needed attending to.

My daughter's friend retiled my bathroom where the carpet had been ripped out. I bought a wig and attempted a few short trips outside the house.

Within a couple of weeks, I was living alone.

It was during this time that I gradually realized I couldn't put the split apart Kathis back together. Part of me had died. Gone was the stink of insecurity that had plagued my former self. Gone were the feelings of worthlessness and fear of the future that had kept me from living my best life. I was proud of who I had become, and my new self thrived. I could do anything I wanted. From now on, I would make the rules, and the first rule was to selfishly take care of myself, and do only those things that were good for me. I deserved that. For too long I'd let people into my life who drug me down, and now finally free, I determined I would surround myself only with positive people. No longer would I tolerate someone's bad moods or anyone who didn't make me smile.

CHAPTER THIRTY-TWO

Recovery

October 21, 2008

I woke slowly, having no reason to hurry. The house was tranquil with the lack of activity.

Quiet as a tomb, I thought.

Nobody mowing their lawn outside, no machines spinning or humming inside. No water running, no ice dumping from the ice maker, not even the heater blowing warm air. Too quiet. My eyes opened, and then closed again, and I listened for the sound of my breathing. It was barely perceptible. Blinking again, I saw my right hand atop my chest, the soft cotton sheet so still beneath it.

I seemed to be dead.

I willed my toes to wiggle, just slightly, enough to reassure me I was still in control of them. Pleased to be among the living, I considered my surroundings. The bed was moved against the far wall, with the window to my right and the door to the stairs on my left. Check. The bathroom door was straight ahead past the foot of the bed. Check. It was all familiar and yet so very different.

I lifted the blankets and stood ghost-like beside the bed. Looking back at it, my body had left only the vaguest of wrinkles. My feet seemed to barely touch the carpet as I walked toward the bathroom, across the rug that covered bloodstains and as I entered the bathroom I avoided looking in the mirror. I didn't want to see my reflection and wasn't completely convinced it would be there anyway.

Every step I took brought the same collage of pictures into my head; the pool of blood, the upturned jewelry box, blood smears on the wallpaper. It wasn't that long ago, but it was past nonetheless, so I wasn't afraid.

Emerging from the bedroom I drifted to the top of the stairs and stopped. Looking down at the tile foyer below, I felt a crushing blow to the top of my head and my legs crumpled under me while I tried in vain to grasp the railing, the balusters, anything, something, to stop myself tumbling down the stairs one by one until, with the dull thud of a watermelon splitting open, my head hit the ceramic tile below. I felt the odd sensation of warm blood mix with the cold of the floor as it oozed around my neck and cheek.

But I was still at the top of the stairs, just looking down. There was no blood. I was still standing, not bleeding to death on the tile below. Sun poured in through the big windows surrounding the front door, the too-green grass and blue sky beyond them still hurt my eyes. Everything was, sort of, as it should be.

Damned, sick thinking.

I wanted it to stop playing with my mind.

October 31, 2008

I woke as usual but as I tried to rise the room spun wildly. An unseen hand pushed my head toward the floor with seemingly massive gravitational pull. My head felt leaden and I was unable to lift it. After a few minutes I fought the heaviness and again tried to sit, but dizziness and nausea crippled me. I reached for the phone by my bed, and called my daughter.

After a repeat MRI the nurses and doctors reassured me I wasn't actively dying. Of course we're all dying, but apparently I wasn't moving toward that target any faster than anyone else. They explained that I was experiencing post-concussive syndrome and post-traumatic stress disorder. The symptoms could last quite some time, they said, up to a year or more. I was given Meclizine for the dizziness, and sent on my way. I supposed having a name for it helped.

#

I died in every possible way, several times a day.

As I drove and another car came toward me, I heard the screech of tires, saw the metal crumple, smelled the burnt rubber and knew I'd died. In a flash of a second, I drove past unscathed.

When I talked with anyone, I couldn't just turn and walk away. I felt them rush after me and stab, shoot, or slam me against a wall. I felt myself fall, bleeding, paralyzed and helpless. I'd shudder, and force myself to continue walking.

As I drove my car onto the arc of a freeway onramp, it crashed through the barrier, launched into space and free floated that interminably long split second until the inevitable impact onto the street below. Smoke and dust rising, my bloody head rested heavily on the horn, the windows shattered with the imprint of my skull. I could see the wreckage. But I continued driving.

Everyone walked too close to me in the grocery store. I particularly hated to pass anyone shopping in the canned food aisle; that 16 oz. can of peaches was a certain weapon. I forced myself to walk past them anyway.

Self-serve gas stations were a godsend, I could sit locked inside the car while the pump ran.

Thankfully, I didn't need to buy anything, because I didn't want to navigate a trip to the mall. There were too many cars and people in one place.

When I did go out I was vigilant, watching everyone, always stealing a look at what they held in their hands. And all the while, I tried to control the thoughts I hoped weren't real.

Most noticeably, no one looked at me. That, too, became worrisome.

Maybe I really was dead. Who is to say I didn't die any one of these times? Maybe there's a period of time when the dearly departed don't know they've crossed over and they live in this sort of unrecognizable limbo where they just keep dying over and over again...until...what? Until a loved one comes to show them the way?

At my one-month checkup I told my doctor that I didn't think I'd had any flashbacks, but that a recording of the whole event continually played in my head, along with a preoccupation with dying in a variety of violent ways. He removed his glasses then patted my hand softly like I was some confused, demented woman and said, "Dear, those *are* flashbacks."

Oh.

Any waking moment of quietude, when I was in my home, or sitting in the parked car, the tape would roll. Always the same, beginning with the night before, it wouldn't stop until the entire tape played, then it would start over again. Talking on the phone, or writing emails, or focusing on paperwork always paused the tape, but it was patient, it lurked in my subconscious until there was nothing to stop it. Then, relentlessly, it began again right where it had left off.

Damn it, this needs to stop.

What I needed was a diversion. I desperately wanted to move forward, and I wanted to have control of my thoughts.

Driving back home that afternoon the gas pedal stuck. The motor raced and my car leapt up the driveway then crashed through the wall of the garage resting inside my broken house. Instantly, I was sitting in the unscathed car, idling in the driveway, as the garage door raised. I got out and yelled, "That's enough! I-AM-NOT-DEAD."

Realizing that my outburst may have been witnessed made me laugh. It felt good. I determined to laugh more often.

I wasn't interested in television, and I hadn't yet gone back to work. I felt well enough once the dizziness passed, but it was intermittent, and I didn't feel safe enough to be taking care of other people. As a result, I had far too much time on my hands with nothing to do. While checking my email account I saw an ad for a dating web site and with Beth's help, I composed a profile.

"Recently widowed, not looking for a relationship, but would like to meet some friends to see a movie now and then or share conversation over an occasional dinner."

I hoped I didn't sound too needy. I attached a picture of me wearing my new wig and sent it off. I suppose I should have added, *"recent head injury, but don't let that concern you."* I hoped I would get a few emails; something to divert my constant obsession with dying.

At home, I opened the doors to the mass of equipment that was a stereo system, previously part of Rod's inner sanctum and off limits to me. I fiddled with the knobs until finally a light came on, then one box emitted music, and I fiddled with the dials until I found a classical radio station.

The music filled me. I danced. Alone, I danced, and sang or hummed along. I cleaned the house and tried to stay busy, and during those times, the tape in my head didn't play.

I knew then that I needed to lean into this thing, in order to take control and rejoin the living. Time may very well heal, but I was already 55 years old, and I wanted to get on with my life.

I went back to the computer and assiduously reviewed my selection criteria on the dating website, added more parameters, and, as was the appropriate action at the time, I contacted a few interesting sounding people on my own. Soon I was anonymously emailing with a variety of very nice people, and the ability to delete them with a single keystroke was very empowering.

After a time, I agreed to meet a couple of them, one, to watch a movie, another I met for a drink. On that website I even met the billionaire who lived at the corner. He invited me to go horseback riding with him; an activity that did as much good for me as any medicine. I always drove my own car to meet them, and never gave my address or contact information. I discovered I had no tolerance for anyone who made me feel the least bit uncomfortable or confused. I found it incredibly easy to select who I wanted to spend time with, and summarily dismissed anyone I didn't.

My sisters worried that I was moving too fast, and urged me to slow down and grieve, but I found little to grieve over, and being with other people kept the slideshow in my head at bay. Besides, the attention was incredibly good for my ego.

As I became more engaged in the world around me, the flashbacks slowed, and soon, I safely returned to work a couple of night shifts per week. Within a year, the flashbacks and slideshow had all but disappeared.

CHAPTER THIRTY-THREE

One Year Later

I met with the police officers a year after Rod "died suddenly." I requested the meeting. I wanted to talk with the officer who had shot Rod and the officers who had found me. The officer who fired the shot was a 23-year veteran of the police force, and until that day, he had never fired his service revolver while on the job.

I thanked all of them for everything they had done. I thanked them for saving me.

I told them had Rod lived he would not have survived prison, or a psychiatric facility, and I wouldn't have felt safe a day that he wasn't locked up. I thanked them again and told them I was proud of them.

As he gripped my hand across the table, the shooter said, "The reason you survived was 99% because of what you did, how you fought back." He had tears in his eyes as he spoke, "We're proud of you, too."

#

Soon after I was released from the hospital, I wrote a note to the 911 operator, framed it, and took it to her office. I dropped the wrapped and tagged package off without meeting her. It read:

"Your steady voice, reassuring words, and the seven minutes of unwavering strength you gave to someone you may never meet, I assure you, will never be forgotten."

A little over a year afterward I met that operator in Rockwall, Texas, at a restaurant near my lake house and we had a drink together. She is a lovely person and we've stayed friends, keeping in touch via Facebook and texts. She keeps those framed words proudly displayed in her living room.

#

The universe seemed to have reset itself when I was almost murdered. I survived, and that, in and of itself was a miracle. Fighting back with every shred of who I was changed me completely. Colors appeared more vivid, foods tasted robust rather than bland. I found my palate could barely tolerate chocolate; the flavor so cloyingly sweet. I am so much stronger, happier, and more at peace than any time in my previous life, and yes, it was a previous life. I have all the memories of that other Kathi; the girl who wasn't taught to value herself, never learned she had a right to seek happiness. Memories of those years appear to me as if I'm looking through a long, hollow tube into someone else's life.

Since The Event, I recognize the inherent evil that manifested in Rod, in my step-father, and in my mother by her complicity and denial. I also recognize how frustrated the therapist must have been, unable to make me see how destructive my life had become, how I had gone from one escape mechanism to another with no break in the pattern. And I now understand how I was able to do what I did that day. In surviving, the best of me was saved, and with it came a great awakening; I was not to mourn a wasted past, but to see through different eyes the great joys life has to offer.

I couldn't have foreseen how dramatically I would change after The Event. Within weeks Janie said she had never known me to be so comfortable in my own skin. Debbie took me to a tarot card reader in New Orleans who, after laying out the first few cards remarked, "I see you are single. I see a recent divorce–I sense that this divorce hit you very hard." I had to laugh at his choice of words.

I sold the big house within six months of The Event. I bought a sailboat, a 25-foot Catalina, and docked it at the marina near my lake house. I named the boat Olive. I met a tall, elegant Englishman who taught me to sail. I loved being on the boat; adjusting the sheets to adapt to changing winds, mindful of what lies below the surface of the water, and always respectful of the weather and its challenges. I learned to navigate a point of sail and capture the wind to make it work for me. Learning to sail was as new as everything else in my life.

My Englishman talks to me about everything, about work, politics, relationships, books; anything and everything. We enjoy each other's company. He is genuinely interested in both our families, and my sisters and friends adore him. He possesses a fabulous sense of humor, and we laugh all the time. He holds my hand. He has the best heart of anyone I have ever met and was horrified when I finally told him what had happened to me. As he gently slid the wig off my head, I cringed and tried to cover my semi-bald head, but he cupped my face in his hands and told me he loved me, had always loved me, then he slowly kissed the lumpy scars on my scalp.

From the moment I met him, I've felt as if I'd known him all my life.

I no longer wonder why these things happened, all that's left now is love and gratitude. I sometimes think about Red; my salvation when I was a young girl. And I often think about that other Horse, the one who *expected nothing less*. I know she would be proud of me.

ABOUT THE AUTHOR

The Olive Picker is Kathryn's first novel. She has previously written *Solitaire*, a short story that was published in The McGuffin magazine in 2006. Her short stories *Hot Lips* and *Runners* were both accepted for online publications in 2005 and 2009 respectively.

Kathryn splits her time between India and Colorado and writes stories about her frequent travels. One of those posts, *Naked Guy,* was published in her hometown Colorado newspaper, The Mountain Connection, in 2013.

Kathryn is very happily married, pursuing her lifelong love of writing, and enjoying life.

She hopes, through her writing, to help people who find themselves in situations of abuse, wherever they are in their journey.

Special acknowledgment and thanks to Vibha Malhotra, founder of Literature Studio, for her advice, constant encouragement, and editing help. Much love and thanks to Peter, who convinced me that people would be interested in my story, then spent hours upon hours reading and proofing the manuscript, but most importantly, because he is my perfect mate.